A DOOR SET OPEN

A DOOR SET OPEN

Grounding Change in Mission and Hope

PETER L. STEINKE

THE
ALBAN
INSTITUTE
HERNDON, VIRGINIA
WWW.ALBAN.ORG

The Alban Institute
2121 Cooperative Way, Suite 100
Herndon, VA 20171

The cartoons that appear on pages 51, 69, and 121 are courtesy of Raymond Johnson. Used with Permission.

Cover design by Tobias Becker, Bird Box Design.

Cover photo by Krista Steinke.

Library of Congress Cataloging-in-Publication Data

Steinke, Peter L.
  A door set open : grounding change in mission and hope / Peter L. Steinke.
     p. cm.
  Includes bibliographical references (p. 135).
  ISBN 978-1-56699-403-3
  1. Church renewal. 2. Mission of the church. 3. Hope--Religious aspects
  --Christianity. 4. System theory. I. Title.
  BV600.3.S736 2010
  262.001'7--dc22
                              2010021121

10   11   12   13   14   VP   5   4   3   2   1

GOOD NEWS: but if you ask me what it is, I know not;
    It is a track of feet in the snow,
It is a lantern showing a path,
    It is a door set open.

                    —G. K. CHESTERTON, "XMAS DAY"

CONTENTS

FOREWORD

I first met Pete Steinke in the fall of 2000 while I was serving as pastor of the Amagansett Presbyterian Church on Long Island, New York. I attended a presbytery-sponsored family systems training event that Pete led called "Bridge Builders." I later took his additional training, "Healthy Congregations." At that time I had no idea that our lives would intersect in a profound way in the future.

Since I held a ThD in clinical pastoral counseling, was a Fellow in the American Association of Pastoral Counselors, and practiced for many years as a pastoral counselor, I came to the conference with a high level of curiosity about what Pete would have to offer regarding how family systems theory might help both conflicted and healthy churches become healthier.

Although already well acquainted with Murray Bowen and Edwin Friedman's work, I had never seen anyone apply family systems principles to faith communities in any concrete, practical, and systematic way before. Pete's seminar took the top of my head off, and I was never the same again. I had finally met a pastor, theologian, and clinical practitioner who really knew the theory and had crafted a vision and practical plan to equip conflicted congregations and their leaders to negotiate the troubled waters of their ecclesial lives and also help nonconflicted churches become healthier.

Pete has been involved in more than two hundred interventions in conflicted churches across the United States in diverse denominational and cultural settings. He has also consulted with several seminaries, from which he has gleaned an unprecedented wealth of experience and knowledge.

In 2003 I was called to be the director of Austin Presbyterian Theological Seminary's Doctor of Ministry program. Remembering that Pete lived in Austin, I contacted him and an endearing friendship began. He gives a three-hour lecture in each of my doctoral seminars, and his three previous books are required reading in my doctoral methods seminar. Students find his books to be invaluable, and he has helped me see that systemic assessment of each congregation must be required in all of our Doctor of Ministry final project proposals.

I later became president of the Association for Doctor of Ministry Education (ADME), an association that represents the 145 Association of Theological Schools' accredited DMin programs in North America, and our board invited Pete to be the keynote speaker for our 2008 annual convention. Our DMin directors were quite taken with Pete's lectures, and he received several invitations to teach DMin courses in various seminaries.

Hearing Pete speak, both in formal lectures and in numerous informal conversations, I saw this current book percolating in him because he kept referencing a salient theme emerging in his work—*mission*. Pete has rightly identified one of the most significant markers of any healthy congregation—a vision and passion for mission. And likewise, he notes how the inverse is equally true—unhealthy churches are usually consumed by anxiety, which causes them to become unduly rigid, self-serving, and inwardly focused.

In this book you will benefit from Pete's extensive inside knowledge of working with both conflicted and healthy congregations as he makes the case that becoming a mission-focused church will improve the systemic health of a congregation. You will find his practical examples both helpful and challenging, his masterful storytelling intriguing, and his theological reflection on the inextricable connections between a biblical commitment to mission and ecclesial systemic health prophetic.

DAVID LEE JONES, THD
Doctor of Ministry Director
Austin Presbyterian Theological Seminary

$\mathcal{A}$CKNOWLEDGMENTS

$\mathcal{A}$ book is a system. Many parts come together and interact to make a whole. I want to thank Beth Ann Gaede and Andrea Lee for their editorial skills and personal patience; their questions, corrections, and suggestions have increased the quality of the content. Serena Verzhinsky should be equally applauded for typing the manuscript. I write in the old-fashioned way, with paper on the table and pen in hand. To decipher my handwriting is a significant task.

Numerous unnamed people from churches in several dozen states and a dozen denominations are contributors. They worked with me in making changes in their congregations. Watching their commitment to the change process and their indefatigable efforts to shift the functioning of their congregations, I marveled. Even the doubters and the fearful ones were instructors, reinforcing the idea of how strong emotional forces can be.

I am grateful to the parish pastors who patiently listened to my insights and compared them to their own situations, namely Bill Knippa, Paul Meyer, Roger Schwarze, Dick Smith, and Bill Snyder. David Jones, president of ADME (Association for Doctor of Ministry Education) offered insight. The wisdom of two judicatory leaders, Debra Rundlett and Cherlynne Beck, helped me see from another angle. My appreciation is deep for the partnership that has formed between Jon Lee, Paul Blom, and myself. They will assist me in a new venture—

NEW VISIONS—in which this book will be vital. New Visions: Leadership for Mission is a training effort to complement the work of church leaders in creating a greater consciousness about mission and broadening the congregation's mission activity.

Finally, I thank my wife, Kelly, who listened to my "Ahas!" and challenged my line of thought. What a system!

INTRODUCTION

I have written this book to encourage and shape a conversation about the church's future in today's world of change and challenge. The first influence on my thinking has been my experience working with churches (1) engaged in conflict, (2) caught in a stubborn impasse, (3) entering a phase of transition, or (4) wanting to sustain a level of effective functioning. Having consulted with more than two hundred churches in eight denominations, ranging in membership from one hundred to six thousand, located in different population areas, I have witnessed both meager efforts and impressive responses to the challenges provoked by change. I will share what I have observed with you.

All congregations are facing challenges brought about by rapid change. But their responses vary greatly, from slight adjustments to surprising adaptations. Why? The late Edwin Friedman, Bowen systems theory advocate and my mentor, used the formula _HE = RO_. Essentially, the formula is shorthand for this rule of thumb: _The hostility (H) of the environment (E) is proportionate to the responses (R) of the organism (O)_. Neither the number nor the strength of the stressors, he contended, creates negative disturbances or personal hardship. The effect of the agitation depends primarily on the individual or group's response to it. Friedman's principle could be expressed as _the challenge of change is equal to the response of the congregation_ (see figure I.1 on page 5).

1

My observations as to what responses most contribute to the challenge of change are noted below. The first three responses have been present in every case.

- Without mature and motivated leaders, little happens.
- Resistance to change is far less intense and protracted when change is made for the sake of mission.
- How emotional processes are understood and handled plays a major role in outcomes.
- Leaders are able to reframe problems as opportunities.
- Leaders can be frozen in their frustration because they do not know how to effect change.
- Good intentions are fortified by good planning and action.
- Mistakes and failures can become learning events.
- Superimposing ideas and formulas to reshape the congregation that have been developed elsewhere can sometimes be helpful. Most effective, however, is the "ground-up" approach in which the congregation takes a course of action that coincides with its own situation and identity.
- People will be more receptive to ideas that are solidly grounded on Scripture and theology.
- People are motivated by both pain and hope.
- Congregations can be trapped in the status quo because they are fundamentally unaware of how societal change has affected the local parish.
- The response to problems may fail because people confuse _adaptive_ problems with _technical_ ones. Instant solutions are substituted for approaches that require continuous learning.
- Clergy leaders—besides being anxious about implementing change for the fear of resistance, removal of support, and so forth—are not well prepared to conduct the change process.
- Transformation involves crisis.

This list contains the key responses congregations have made to meet the challenge of change. Later in the book, I will highlight many of these items in descriptions of several congregations.

The second contribution to my thoughts about the challenge of change comes from the theology of hope. Hope provides a new angle of vision. When things look bleak or unmovable, hope sees more than what is there. If congregations are to respond to the challenge of change, halfhearted actions will not achieve what is desired. Victim thinking will only reinforce a sense of powerlessness. Hope can carry a congregation over the threshold of "can't." A friend of mine teaches in the social sciences at a university in Kentucky. For her doctoral dissertation, she studied African American families in parts of Indiana and Kentucky to ascertain why some families broke the cycle of poverty, yet most stayed mired in their poor conditions. The repeat families did not believe they had any strengths; thus they felt helpless, powerless, and hopeless. This attitude can affect organizations, too: "There is nothing we can do." But hope puts possibility into play. Hope is a concrete invitation to act in adventurous ways.

Even more, the church has neglected a central teaching of the Bible that is the very foundation of Christian hope. The Bible assures us that God will create a new earth on which we will live in resurrected bodies. Theologian Anthony Hoekema explains, "The kingdom of God . . . does not mean merely the salvation of certain individuals nor even a chosen group of people. It means nothing less than the complete renewal of the entire cosmos, culminating in the new heaven and the new earth."[1]

If God indeed has the whole world in his hands and plans, God's redemption is far more than me and my salvation. The resurrection has changed the course of history and the cosmos. God is present in the world to renew it, just as he is present in calling the believer to be a contributor to the divine renewal by loving and serving people. And our lives of love and service become, in the words of theologian Miroslav Volf, the "building materials" for that new earth. Our hope in God's new kingdom can create an exciting and meaningful way of life. "Hope is a way of imaging God's future and persevering in faith that it will arrive," writes New Testament professor Sarah Henrich.[2] Defining hope in this manner, hope—however tenuous—is the conviction that our longing will eventually be satisfied. The definition embraces the idea that longings draw us toward the future, direct our focus, arouse our passion, and impart meaning to our actions. Augustine, in his famous phrase—"Thou has formed us for Thyself, and our hearts are restless till they find rest in Thee"[3]—grounds the deep yearning in the God of promise who is responsive to human needs.

The third source of influence on my thinking lies in the theoretical realm, systems theory, which I have written about in other Alban publications. It is a way of viewing the world, of understanding human interaction, and of seeing how emotional processes guide behavior. Especially pertinent to this discourse are a number of Edwin Friedman's insights and Murray Bowen's concepts not incorporated in my earlier books, such as "imaginative gridlock" (Friedman) and the "societal emotional process" (Bowen). For those who might not be acquainted with this theory, I have listed representative views of system thinking:

- Nothing is known in itself, apart from connectedness.
- The whole cannot be understood by simply understanding each part.
- One focuses on the relationships among discrete parts, not on separate parts alone.
- Behavior is mutually reinforced. Nothing is influenced in one direction.
- Make one change in the system and other changes have to happen.
- During periods of change and challenge, emotional processes (automatic behaviors) increase.
- No emotional system will change unless people in the system change how they function with one another.

FIGURE I.1. FRIEDMAN'S FORMULA: *HE = RO*

The horizontal axis represents the severity of environmental conditions; the vertical axis represents maturity of the response. In the illustration below, Quadrant 1 contains a small percentage of people who are capable and well-balanced individuals experiencing little stress in their environment. Quadrant 2 represents people who are quite reactive even though the stressors in their lives are low. In Quadrant 3, we see mature people who use their responses to handle life well, even stress and negativities. But Quadrant 4 encompasses people who lack the skills to deal with severe conditions; their behavior is typically erratic, evasive, and irresponsible.

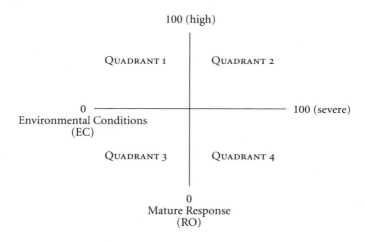

Bowen believed it took at least four years to change a family's emotional processes—and change wasn't guaranteed. Imagine the time that may be required to change a larger institution. Attention to emotional process is essential in working with change.

By combining my experience with the theology of hope and systems thinking, I want to engage you in thinking about your congregation, the challenges of change it faces, and the opportunity to take new direction and action. Ultimately, I hope you will gather others in the discussion to enrich the congregation's mission and ministry.

Part I

The Context

EVERYONE NOW AGREES that we are at a new season in the life of the North American church, a new season that is starkly different from what was but that has almost taken us by surprise. That new season of dislocation is surely to be seen as a profound challenge to the church. It is, moreover, widely felt, not without reason, to be <u>an invitation for newness together</u> that moves past old postures that predictably, perhaps inevitably, produced quarrels. The massive and unarguable dislocation of the conventional church may be an occasion for <u>a common resubmission to the power of God's spirit</u>.

—WALTER BRUEGGEMANN
Deep Memory, Exuberant Hope

Chapter 1

There Once Was a World

*A*t a workshop I was leading, a woman stood up and said, "If 1950 were to return, my congregation would be ready." Succinctly, she summarized a nagging problem for many churches. <u>The context in which congregations now find themselves is quite different from 1950</u>. "How we do church," though, has been quite persistent: Become a member of the local congregation, contribute money and effort, participate in communal events, volunteer time and goods, and worship regularly or at least several times a year. This pattern of "church" continued for decades in North America, but then things changed quickly. *s. "American Grace"*

<u>There once was a world</u> where the church functioned according to what some have called <u>the "attractional" model</u> X (others have named it the participatory model). People come to a place, consume the spiritual goods, and serve as patrons to "meet the budget." But a shift has happened. North American culture took new turns. Church consultant Anthony Robinson observed: "Many dis-spirited, bewildered, paddling-as-fast-as-we-can, struggling or conflicted congregations have come to believe that what they are undergoing is about them. 'We are a bad church' or a dying church, or a failing church. . . . <u>Much of what's being faced and experienced by many mainline Protestant churches is not about them</u>. <u>It is about the end of an era</u>, a sea change in the religious ecology of North America and the role of

congregations in our society. American Christendom is over."[1]
Christendom refers to a period of time when the Christian faith
profoundly informed the culture. And, in turn, the culture carried the traditions, symbols, and rituals of the Christian faith.
Another often-used term—*post-Christian era*—captures the reality that the importance and influence of Christianity in North
American society has been in decline for at least three decades.
In a "post-Christian" world, the church cannot expect favorable
treatment or higher visibility.

One could say that a gathering storm—a confluence of fac-
tors—has assailed the church and its dominant perch on the
societal ladder. None of this has to do with the church's internal
functioning. The sea change is external or contextual. There
once was a world that was eager to be hospitable to Christian
churches and supported "blue laws," soccerless Sundays, eating
fish rather than meat on Friday, public prayer in schools and at
nodal events, deferring to clergy by way of discounts, weekly
religion sections in urban newspapers, and greeting others with
"Merry Christmas."

The Background

Psychology has told us that what we are looking at is always affected by its background. We can better understand the church's
challenge by looking at the backdrop—the world itself. What
are the changing conditions that call for a new response?

To initiate a discussion about today's challenges, I present a
number of forces that confront today's church. The list is not in
any order of importance and is not exhaustive. I have selected
ones that would help you see the breadth of the challenges the
church faces. The church lives in a new context, especially one
marked by a pace of change never seen before. Other institutions like family, education, business, medicine, law, and politics
confront changes in their respective roles. All institutions are
exploring how to respond to changing conditions. Examine what

I present here, and perhaps you will add an emerging force of your own in your discussions.

Postmodern Philosophy

Postmodernism is a set of ideas that basically says we live in a strange universe. No grand narrative centers life. One world view is as acceptable as another. Any claim that one's theoretical framework is true for all is disregarded. Pluralism is extolled, and differences are celebrated. No single morality takes center stage. All absolutes are relative. Basically, the world is disenchanted of its reliability and coherence.

Dogmatic Atheism

Some atheists (Christopher Hitchens, Sam Harris, and Richard Dawkins, to name a few) have formed strong arguments about the dark side of religion, and they push for its nonessential role. They see religion as a perpetrator of violence and an inhibitor of rational decision making. A leftover from prescientific days, they argue, religion continues its delusion that life has purpose and a goal. "God" is a hypothesis that has failed. The world has come to a point where God is unnecessary. "The mainline churches have a real problem on their hands," world religion scholar Huston Smith declares. "Bluntly stated, it is atheism."[2]

Supermodernity

Less frequently discussed than postmodernism is French social critic Marc Auge's speculation that the present world is shaped by "supermodernity," a crisis in social relations and the search for meaning. Auge explains supermodernity with two ideas— *nonplaces* and *superabundance*. Non-places are spaces designed for anonymity, passing through, and nonengagement. Auge states, "A space which cannot be defined as relational, historical, or concerned with identity will be a non-place."[3] Counted among non-places are supermarkets, malls, superhighways, outlets, large hotels, airports, cineplexes, condo complexes, even ATM cash machines and fast food franchises. If not focused on relationships, megachurches can be non-places. Little human association happens in these places. They are controlled environments intended to meet the instrumental needs of private individuals. Disappearing are places intended for relationships, such as churches and civic groups. Few places remain where people can find community, meaning, and hope. The other feature of supermodernity is superabundance. An excess of events begs for our attention, but who has time to reflect on each one? To discern the meaning of an event is impossible when, the very next day, new events sweep over us. When excess combines with acceleration, no time is available for deliberating and musing. Everything becomes impermanent, fleeting, and remains unexamined. *Flying Through an asteroid field*

Science and Religion

Some attribute religion's decline to the elevation of science as the master of truth. Huston Smith notes that "The biologist E. O. Wilson says that the struggle for the human soul in the twenty-first century will be between science and religion."[4]

Bryan Appleyard, former science columnist for the *London Times* and author of *Understanding the Present: Science and the Soul of Modern Man*, pictures science "colonizing the entire world, including its religions."[5] Since everything in life tends to enlarge itself, he thinks science's hegemony will continue to flourish.

Some scientists believe religion is a leftover from the epistemology of the past. Once science is capable of determining "what is," religion will be a relic of the past, centered in feeling and inspiration and having nothing to do with objective reality. "The universe," one scientist said, "has no meaning." Evolutionary psychologist Robert Wright pronounces, "We are built to be effective animals, not happy ones."

Those who employ the scientific method claim the only way to discover the truth about the hidden universe is to maintain an objective, impersonal, and dispassionate role. One is an observer of what is. Nonetheless, the religious method (if one could call it that) invites one to become a participant in life, being personal and passionate. One searches for what might be. So we are presented two fundamental choices: The first is a vision of a material universe in which life suddenly emerged, evolved by chance happenings, and is destined for nowhere. Even then, if you leave the biological sciences for the physical sciences, the law of entropy says the cosmos is headed for disorder and death. Religion, though, contains a vision of the universe moving toward renewal, where the human longings for peace, community, and justice find completion.

When I was consulting at St. Mark's Cathedral in Seattle, I discovered their Sunday evening compline service, which is attended by five to six hundred people weekly. A large contingency is youth and young adults. A lay leader at the cathedral jested that they came often because it was a cheap date. The evening I attended, I sat next to a young woman in her late twenties. She had small streaks of orange in her hair and one pierced ear with a pendant earring. During compline, I failed to stand immediately when the rest of the congregation did, and she nudged me. "We stand for the Apostles' Creed." Thanking her, I rose. I recited the creed. She stared silently into the dark space of the cavernous cathedral. When I left, I asked her if she came to compline often. "Yes," she answered, "I come as often as I can." The conversation ceased for a couple of minutes as we maneuvered our way out of the building. Suddenly she said, "I don't give two shits about religion. Weird, I guess." When I asked why she came, she explained, "I'm looking for something more in my life." And she darted off to meet a friend. I am sure she wouldn't call "something more in my life" mystery, the Holy, or transcendence, but her longing wasn't about what is. Albert Einstein, the physical scientist, remarked that imagination is more important than knowledge, for while knowledge points to what is, imagination points to all that will be. In a society bent on immediate outcomes and tangible results, science delivers. As a world view, however, science is mute and dumb.

The Neuro Society

One part of science almost completely overlooked in conversations about new challenges to the church is the "neuro revolution." The brain, Edwin Friedman liked to point out, is our largest secreting organ. It is a chemicalcopia. Neuroscience promises to give us more tools to control our mental and emotional processes. If brain chemistry is in charge of those processes, all one has to do is rework the chemical equation to change them. "Neuroenhancement" is the use of chemicals to stimulate brain function for nonmedical purposes. "By providing new tools to influence human emotion, cognition and sensory systems," Zack Lynch, director of the Neurotechnology Industry Organization, asserts, "neurotechnology will create profound consequences in how we perceive social, political and cultural problems."[6] How neuroscience could affect religious lives is being equally explored, such as replacing anxiety with a calmness, substituting doubt with confidence, and exchanging alienation with a sense of oneness. Spirituality could be about chemistry alone, if spirituality is primarily thought of as enjoying positive feelings and less strain.

The Ghost of Gnosticism

A small group of first-century Christians put forth a world view quite different from the mainstream. It was called gnosticism. *Gnosis* is a Greek word signifying "knowledge." Its negative—*ag-*

nostic, meaning "not knowing," may be a more familiar term. But the knowledge of the Gnostics isn't about factual data or general information; it is knowledge acquired only through enlightenment. Gnosticism could be thought of as illumination (light, insight), inspiration (inner light), and liberation (freedom from ignorance). Salvation is shaking off ignorance and gaining special knowledge through a certain amount of effort and diligence. Some view gnosticism as a forerunner of the "new thought" in the West, which urges the use of the mind to control life events. If we can visualize what we want, we can achieve our desired outcome. Its current manifestations are easily seen in a plethora of New Age publications. But it is also edging its way into traditional Christian circles, most notably the "prosperity gospel." Positive thinking prepares our mind for success, and God wants to bless us abundantly. The "good news" of prosperity is that any day now we will enjoy the abundant life. God is portrayed as a rich investor in our stock, with nothing more in mind than to manage our portfolio, a bull market for life. To upgrade our life, all we need to do is think "positively" and "really want it," for what we can see in our mind, we can produce in our life. Some have dubbed it "the claim-it-and-have-it" theology, but positive attitude is the bottom line. *Joel Osteen*

This is quite seductive for struggling churches because the prosperity churches are growing. Maybe a little more sunshine and some "you can do it" messages would draw more folks into the fold. Kate Bowler, a doctoral candidate at Duke University, has examined the teachings of the largest rapidly growing churches. Three of the twelve largest churches in the nation are proponents of the prosperity gospel. Fifty of the largest 260 churches in this country are prosperity oriented.[7] Headed by market-savvy pastors, these churches have the same upbeat, positive message, with God as the divine Daddy Bucks. All you need is the right mind, the right attitude, the right effort, because you will never get that Rolls Royce with a bicycle mind.

Therapeutic Dominance

A number of years ago, psychologist Philip Rieff wrote *The Triumph of the Therapeutic*. He remarked that people today regard satisfaction as more significant than salvation. Today's big religious question, he argued, is not "Can I be saved?" but "Does it feel right?" To accommodate the modern soul, preachers have volunteered to oversee the gentrification of the "old God" of sin and grace. Designed for the American consumer, the new god is like a giant Prozac or a sweetener. God will help you improve yourself, give you tips on reducing stress in your life, and offer a Scripture-based set of coping skills with satisfaction guaranteed.

Satisfaction as redemption is what theologian Shirley Guthrie had in mind in his critique of the "candy machine God." God has become a dispenser of goodies to indulge our appetites, champion our causes, or steady our nerves. But Guthrie believed that the Holy One had more important things to do than spend time doting on our transient happiness. Guthrie announced frankly, the candy machine doesn't exist.[8]

Ralph Wood, professor of religion and literature at Baylor University, called the devotion to satisfaction "kiddianity." As people slide back into their childish hungers for immediate gratification, acceptance, and emotional uplifts, there is no end to the preachers who will sweeten the sour apple. No darkness. No delays. No frustration. This fits well with the prosperity gospel. To gain your desired bonanza, it is essential to ban thoughts of the defeated life.

The triumph of the therapeutic means the culture of immediate pleasure prevails over the culture of hope. Of course, no one is against comfort and contentment. I believe, though, they come as a byproduct, not a direct hit. Easter joy is a surprise. It follows the Friday of forsakenness and humiliation. Without the cross, the best therapeutic theology can offer is cheap grace. Exiled from Eden, Adam and Eve landed in a swamp, not in a pot of gold or in the fountain of youth.

Almost a century ago, Aldous Huxley wrote his novel *Brave New World*. To satirize his own day, he imagined a twenty-fifth-century society devoid of any dissatisfaction. The quest for contentment was satisfied by the wonders of chemistry, specifically a drug labeled "Soma." The miracle drug cast out misery and provided a whole range of delights. What concerned Huxley was the possibility that people would give up their freedom to stay in the stupor of serenity. Forsaking their thought processes, the "somatized" people would become satisfaction addicts.

The Response

Like other organizations, the church is being significantly affected by swift social changes, and the impact is receiving public attention. Joseph Bottum, editor of the journal *First Things*, contends that "the Great Church of America has come to an end," meaning the mainline churches. Noting that the high-water mark for Sunday worship attendance came around 1965, Bottum "sees nothing but continual leakage" in mainline churches. If the present trend continues, by the year 2020 another 15 to 20 percent shrinkage will occur.[9] By the year 2050, researcher David Olson foresees the loss of fifty-five thousand congregations.[10]

Strangely, interest in spiritual things is high, but people are not necessarily seeking them in churches. When a report indicated that the percentage of North Americans identifying themselves as Christian fell ten points between 1989 and 2009, Jon Meacham, editor of *Newsweek* magazine, wrote an article entitled "The End of Christian America."[11] Not too long ago, more than half of North Americans reported they were members of mainline Protestant churches.

Rapid Change

Today's rapidly changing world is pressing the church to respond to a shift of paradigms—but not for the first time. In previous

shifts, the church has both responded slowly and responded
imaginatively. More than once, much of what people have
thought and done has had to be reworked. As the Jesus movement spread beyond Israel into the first-century Mediterranean
world, profound Jewish traditions had to be examined. Questions about how to handle the Hellenistic influence required new
thinking. A second-century bishop named Marcion separated
from the mainstream church. Hostile to the Old Testament,
Marcion argued that the God spoken of there was different
from the God of the New Testament. In the sixteenth century,
the Copernican revolution brought about new thinking in the
church regarding the cosmos and people's place in it. In that
same era, the sale of indulgences became a tipping point for
the breakdown of the Western church. In more recent times,
the ongoing tension between science and religion has required
new thinking.

Each shift carried both danger and opportunity. In today's
context, the church is challenged by the astonishing pace of
change in the world. We are in some ways ill prepared to act
rapidly, since the church is as an entity made up of people who
are creatures of nature, subject to seasons, rhythms, and stages.
We cannot be mechanically geared for shifting quickly.

Regardless of the nature of change, the church affirms that
the God of Abraham, Isaac, and Jacob is the God who has been
active in history and who will be active in the future. Faced with
a strange, new world, the church is challenged to be true to its
purpose and attuned to its context. I believe the paradigm shift
of rapid change constitutes a rich *opportunity* for the church.
God has set the door open to the future. God's future arrives
in the person of Jesus Christ. The church's response to God's
restoration of the whole creation through Jesus is the vocation
to which we are called. N. T. Wright, a New Testament scholar,
states it eloquently: "But new creation has already begun. The
sun has begun to rise. Christians are called to leave behind, in

the tomb of Jesus, all that belongs to the brokenness and in-completeness of the present world. It is time, in the power of the Spirit, to take up our proper role, our fully human role, as agents, heralds, and stewards of the new day that is dawning. That, quite simply, is what it means to be Christian: to follow Jesus Christ into the new world, God's new world, which he has thrown open before us."[12]

But the new day is as perplexing as it is promising. "It is abundantly and unmistakably clear that we are in a deep dislo-cation in our society," Old Testament scholar Walter Bruegge-mann explains, "that touches every aspect of our lives."[13] We are living in a new context where old certainties are disappearing, old institutions are less dependable, old assumptions are ques-tionable, and old neighborhoods are less cohesive. Of course, the dislocation touches the church. Brueggemann names a few of these dislocations: "bewilderment about mission," "mean-spirited dispute," and "anxieties about members and growth."

Logically, if not spiritually, we may even have to allow for the possibility that these dislocations could be part of God's new creation. It may be God working through the unknown that contributes to the destabilization of the world. God is no stranger to Eden's deportation, Babel's scattering, the exodus, the exile, and crucifixion. God can be surprising, mysterious, taking history into unexpected turns.

CHAPTER 2

EMOTIONAL SYSTEMS
AND THE NEW ANXIETY

Change is a magnet for emotional reactions. Anxiety becomes more intense. Yet I cannot conceive of any clergy or lay leaders bringing about change successfully, apart from knowing and handling emotionality. Let's look at emotional systems and how they function during periods of change. To avoid confusion, I need to define two terms: *emotional* and *new anxiety*. In Bowen systems theory, *emotional* describes automatic human behavior. Feelings are part of the emotional process, but the emotional process does not consist entirely of feelings. Emotionality is a hard-wired, built-in force designed to be part of human survival equipment. Emotional behavior includes all of the mechanisms that are used to maximize security (feelings and morals; the drive to obtain water and food, territory, and shelter). Automatic behaviors contribute to the same end—survival. Consequently, reflexive actions are more evident when our survival is threatened. When our anxiety is high, survival instincts act not only quickly but also forcefully.

What I call the *new anxiety* is essentially intense anxiety. Highly agitated anxiety produces excessive apprehension. Surely, another shoe is going to fall soon. The new anxiety distorts reality. What is imagined or expected to happen is not proportionate to the threat. Aggravating it all, we sense we will not be able to influence events or outcomes, rendering us apathetic souls. The new anxiety can also erupt into sudden aggression as a defense

21

against even minor uncertainties. <u>The new anxiety promotes more intense and frequent reactivity</u>. People are less able to regulate themselves. <u>Instinctive actions prevail over thoughtful choices</u>. Path A in figure 2.1 is followed more often than path B.

FIGURE 2.1. REACTION OR RESPONSE

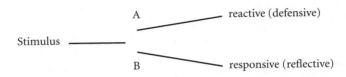

Emotional Processes

Many commentators are probing the challenge of change for churches. Acknowledging the critical condition in which the church finds itself, both externally and internally, they sound the alarm and suggest the kinds of changes needed. Oddly, few address how the change process itself works. Consideration of emotional processes receives scant attention, if any. Whether the discussion is about the church growth movement or finding the congregational "code," exploring the emergent church or focusing on discipleship, becoming part of the missional renaissance or hitting the "bulls-eye," the conversation proceeds as if the emotional system is irrelevant to it all.

Emotionality

Nothing has been more helpful to me in serving congregations than recognizing and understanding <u>congregations as emotional systems</u>. My understanding is constantly put to the test. Wise as I think I may be, I am still caught off guard by emotional reactions. In church conflicts, I introduce a process to bring about change so that anxiety in the system leads to (and does not block) new learning. To accomplish it, I expect fair play, goodwill, and integrity. Without them, the antagonisms have no antidote. Nonetheless, I run into the emotional buzzsaw of sabotage. In one respect, I anticipate the underhanded attempts to discredit the process or myself. Sometimes, the sabotage comes from charm, not aggression, making it even harder to detect. To a degree, I appreciate the sabotage, because it indicates that the process is working for the benefit of the whole and not for some self-interest group. When people feel they are losing control or not getting from the process what they want, they try to disrupt or dishonor what is happening.

What surprises me most is the deceit to which some will resort to have it their way. Often, they hide their dishonesty under a patina of piety: "No one wants reconciliation more than we do." Meanwhile, they disseminate false information or withhold information to bolster their side of the rift. I have confronted leaders about their dissembling. Typically, they turn it around, saying I am listening to the other side too much, or the other side is even more guilty of the same behavior. When the survival brain goes to work, the thinking brain isn't open for business. *

While I attempt to stay outside of the emotionality, I am not immune to it. I have to examine my own survival impulses. Eager to do well, I have to ask myself why I may dislike someone, or why a backside comment disturbs me. Often, I open myself to the observation of others to learn about my behavior. I am under no illusions—emotional processes are absolutely powerful. I need self-awareness in order to make choices about my actions, or my own emotionality will prevail.

With either stuck or transitional churches (churches troubled more by uncertainty than polarization), I have been sidetracked by participants' dissociating (acting as if nothing happens) rather than dissembling. I find myself working with leaders who refuse to make timely or necessary decisions. Afraid of splintering the congregation or offending a block of key members, church leaders allow crucial matters to hang in the air. They can easily attack me for not providing them sufficient information or solving their predicament. Even though I never contract for that purpose, leaders excuse their own indecision by outsourcing blame. Clearly, the leaders are afraid of the emotional side of congregations. But Kathy Wiseman, a faculty member at the Bowen Center who works with family businesses, told me that, when I work with anxious systems, I need to remember my emotional functioning contributes to the outcome of the process, either negatively or positively. If I am leading a group toward more calm reflectiveness as they make important decisions, I need to be able to regulate myself (as I would have them do with themselves). For me to be as anxious as they may be is to leave the group leaderless. One cannot be a leader and be as anxious as everyone else. Sabotage need not come from others. My own reactivity can do it.

When the challenge of change confronts a congregation, members' survival brains surely will excite their emotional forces. Supervised by the amygdala (the anxiety alarm in the brain), a rapid line of defense takes over in threatening situations. The amygdala functions to protect an organism by

- appraising danger and acting faster than consciousness,
- operating apart from awareness,
- eliminating any set of options that might delay action,
- generalizing for rapid reaction,
- pairing an outside threat with any previous thought, feeling, or prior experience.

Fully operative at birth, the amygdala has no sense of time (a past stimulus can retrigger anxiety at any time). Actually, the amygdala is interested in two things: (1) will something harm or injure me, or (2) will it annihilate me? This prepackaged instinct can lock up the whole brain so that only its survival strategies matter.

Homeostasis

Emotional processes, once repeated, can become patterned. We react to one another's words or actions in predictable ways. For example, one group of people may withdraw in the face of angry expressions. On the other hand, a second group may fight fire with fire, exchanging volatile comments. Either way, the processes, if continually repeated, become emotionally set in place. This preference for coherence and stability has been named *homeostasis*, literally, "to function in the same way." We like the familiar, the matter of fact, and the known. ✱

Edwin Friedman uses the phrase "the persistence of form" to convey the same phenomenon. He offered three concepts—*emotional barriers*, *imaginative gridlock*, and *resistance*—to explain why systems persist in their old form or pattern, even more so with the new anxiety.

Emotional Barriers

Friedman defines an emotional barrier as "an artificial limit born of mythology and preserved by anxiety." In other words, an unquestioned belief, kept in place by tradition or anxiety, predetermines what is seen, understood, and believed. For instance, the myth of four humors in medicine retarded advancements for centuries. Scientific opinion blamed disease on the imbalance of body fluids. The germ theory of disease had to overcome the emotional barrier of medical practitioners who stood to lose trust and respect for defending the body fluid theory. It took the invention of the microscope to shatter the four humors barrier.

Friedman's prime example of an emotional barrier involved a whole continent. In *A Failure of Nerve*, he suggests that Europe, near the beginning of the 1400s, was emotionally stuck. Europe was a civilization with a pinched vision. It may even have been corporately depressed. A combination of events had led to the malaise: The continent was emerging from the Dark Ages, the feudal system was breaking down, and the death blows of the Black Plague had eliminated nearly half of the population. Trapped in its own corruption, the ecclesiastical establishment was in no position to unite society, much less inspire it. Friedman noted that the scientific community had been in an exhausted state for nearly a millennium. And the common complaints of every era—economic chaos, social unrest, greed, moral decay, taxes, profiteering—led one observer to conclude that the end of the fifteenth century was "a bad time for humanity." Historian Barbara Tuchman said institutions failed, and towns, divided by class war, were embroiled in hostilities. Citizens struggled with a universe without purpose, events beyond their control, and an absence of stability and order. But Tuchman's review of fifteenth-century Europe revealed an unexplained change of events. She said, "[At] some imperceptible moment, by some mysterious chemistry, energies were refreshed, ideas broke out of the mold of the Middle Ages into new realms, and humanity found itself redirected."[1]

Friedman attributed the flourishing of the arts, the energizing of science, and the general kindling of imagination to the astounding discovery of the "New World." Europe's inventiveness was excited. No longer was the equator thought to be the end of the earth, for explorers had passed it and had made a turn around Cape Horn, even as European explorers had sailed westward discovering a land unthought of.

With Europe bursting with creative force, the church woke up. Martin Luther translated the Bible into the people's language, breaking the emotional barrier of the bureaucratic church's hold on Holy Writ. Similarly, people were reminded that they were part of the "royal priesthood." Long considered to be the clergy's monopoly, access to God became open to all. Each person could now approach the Divine without the mediation of a priest.

Imaginative Gridlock

Friedman's second concept involves human survival instincts. During anxious periods, what is most needed—imagination—is most unavailable. Reacting supersedes thoughtfulness. Anxiety locks up the imagination and misplaces the key. One's imaginative capacities are stillborn. For one thing, without the conscious mind, we are not able to enlarge the list of possibilities. We become prisoners of our shortsightedness.

Anxiety, at least for the moment, suspends imagination, as the ensuing story reveals. The hot, dry summer of 1949 in Montana left the grasslands vulnerable to fire. Sure enough, an infectious fire ignited in Mann Gulch. Transported by helicopter, firefighter Wagner Dodge and about a dozen fire jumpers were airlifted and dropped in the area to combat what had become an inferno. The gulch divided the pine trees from the grasslands. Dodge instructed the men to go to the river, about two hundred yards away. Evening approached and the winds quickly reversed, sending balls of flame from the treetops across the gulch onto the parched grasslands. As the firefighters backtracked, the flames created a wall of fire that was moving toward them. Knowing they could not get to the river ahead of the fire, Dodge stopped. He ordered his men to do the same. In panic, they kept moving. Some ran straight for the water; some ascended a grassy hillside. Dodge started to burn the grasses below him and stomped on them. He spread himself on the parched ground, putting a handkerchief wetted with water on his forehead for oxygen. Dodge survived. Only two other firefighters lived.

Under severe conditions, Dodge broke the gridlock of his own initial instincts. He eliminated the fire-enabling grasslands where he stood. Later, one of the survivors who had seen Dodge stop told investigators that he thought Dodge "had gone nuts." In the same investigation, Dodge was asked why the others had bypassed his orders. Dodge replied that they lost "attention," having only one thing in mind.[2] They were imaginatively gridlocked. As we might say today, Dodge acted counterintuitively. With his own fears no longer useful, Dodge thought of an alternative.

Resistance

Friedman insists that resistance to change, a third contributor to homeostasis, is a natural phenomenon. He underscored the significance of resistance in his own parable of plumbing:

> Underneath every sink is a well-known vertical looped cylinder. The purpose of the pipe, called a trap, is to prevent noxious gases from entering the system. Every time it fills up or "chokes" on the influx, it saves the house and ultimately the entire network. But now let us animate those pipes. Suppose one of those traps under a sink decided to straighten itself out. We may well imagine the increased anxiety in the others. Some of which might well "go through the roof." And it would seem right to conjecture that they would do everything they could to pressure that newly autonomous pipe not to straighten itself out; or, if that were too late, to bend it back in shape (out of shape?) again.[3]

Emotional resistance to change is powerful. In our minds is this formula: Stability equals safety. The amygdala is keyed to suddenness and newness, for either could be threatening.

Since the amygdala is ready to react if something is strange, new, or novel, resistance serves as a defensive action, usually apparent in sabotaging behavior. Friedman called dealing with resistance "the key to the kingdom." Minimal reaction to the resisting positions of others, whether exhibited in apathy or aggression, is "the key." "It is simply not possible to succeed at the effort of leadership through self-differentiation without trig-gering reactivity. The capacity of a leader to be prepared for, to be aware of, and to learn how to . . . deal with this type of crisis (sabotage) may be the most important aspect of leadership. It is literally the key to the kingdom."[4] If the leader stays the course without compromising, abandoning, or corrupting the goal, good outcomes, though not guaranteed, are more apt to happen.

The Sanballat Maneuver

As the leader embarks on a visionary path or a truth-telling venture, subversive forces use fear, threat, and accusation to derail the leader from the path. The leader's temptation is to restore the togetherness and tranquility, forsaking the change and the visionary path, or, at best, pandering to the resistors and dampening the challenge of change.

Having heard me speak on leadership and sabotage at a work-shop, a participant suggested that I read Nehemiah 6:1–15, a story of a leader's self-regulation when under attack in the midst of change. Nehemiah had proposed a vision for the people of Israel, securing the holy city Jerusalem with a shield of brick and stone. His leadership and vision in completing the walls created strong reactivity. Sanballat, Tobiah, and Geshem requested to meet with Nehemiah alone. Recognizing their nefarious intentions, he refused to go see them. Unsuccessful in detour-ing Nehemiah, they sent an open letter to be read in public to incite doubt and fear among the people. Accusing Nehemiah of seditious activity and self-aggrandizement, Sanballat set out to undermine Nehemiah's leadership. Isn't Nehemiah, Sanballat intimates, another manipulative, untrustworthy leader?

Nehemiah responds to Sanballat's letter in terse terms: "Nothing like what you are saying is happening; you are just making it up out of your head." Then he notes, "They were all trying to frighten us, thinking, 'Their hands will get too weak for the work, and it will not be completed.'" (Neh. 6:8–9). He stayed on course, tapped into his emotional stamina, stood on his principles, and asked God for strength. So when the next threat came—a death threat, no less—Nehemiah asked, "Should a man like me run away?" (Neh. 6:11). He did not. "So the wall was completed on the twenty-fifth of Elul, in fifty-two days" (Neh. 6:15).

A natural response of any emotional system is to return to its previous state when challenged and strained. After the initial steps toward change, a leader will therefore encounter resistance, mostly from those who are emotionally invested. As Friedman noted, such resistance is predictable: "Most theories of leadership recognize the problem of mistakes, but there is a deeper systemic phenomenon that occurs when leaders do precisely what they are supposed to do—lead."[5] People who can differentiate well—act maturely—will arouse anxiety in less mature people.

The ensuing sabotage is sometimes organized and sometimes just mindless opposition. The challenge to the leader is to self-regulate in the midst of anxious reactivity. Being focused on principle and direction, the leader does not get caught up on rash behaviors or cruel comments. As a last resort, reactors will demonize the leader (twisting the strengths of differentiation into the weakness of self-absorption). Friedman comments:

> As they did with Columbus, such persons (saboteurs) will describe well-differentiated leaders as compulsive rather than persistent, as obsessive rather than committed, as foolhardy rather than brave, as a dreamer rather than imaginative, as simple-minded rather than dedicated, as inflexible rather than principled, as hostile rather than aggressive, as bullheaded rather than resolute, as desperate rather than inspired, as autocrats rather than tough-minded, as ambitious rather than courageous, as domineering rather than self-confident, as egotistical rather than self-assured, as selfish rather than self-possessed, and as unfeeling, insensitive, callous, and cold rather than determined.

And they will cloak their sabotage with the banner of the cherished virtues of safety and togetherness.[6]

<u>Leading change brings out both reactive forces and responsive ones</u>. But once anxiety runs a high fever, Friedman says, one can never rely on insight or reasonableness or even love. That's not part of the repertoire of the amygdala. Imagine Moses urging any of the three in his request to Pharaoh to let the Israelites go. Pharaoh is only capable of reacting, raising the ante—"make more bricks." <u>Emotional wisdom would have any leader rely more on one's own responses than changing others' reactions</u>.

CHAPTER 3

SO THAT YOU MAY
HOPE AGAIN

W e have explored how difficult change can be in an emotional system. Yet the conversation would be incomplete without a discussion of the role of hope in the change process, that something new is possible. In *Change or Die*, Alan Deutschman, senior editor of the magazine *Fast Company*, sets forth a new model for the change process. In doing so, he mentions hope, or similar ideas, more than thirty times. Deutschman states, "The real key is to give people hope, not facts."[1] Following up this thought, he says, "The first key to change isn't offering protection or admonition." What counts is "inspiring hope" so that people believe and expect that they can and will change their lives.[2] Yet again, he claims, "The first key to change is: you form a new emotional relationship with a person or a community that inspires and sustains hope."[3]

For the purposes of this discussion, we will look at hope in the context of God's people in exile, a time of dislocation and near despair, like ours. They are emotionally drained, at a low ebb. Along comes Isaiah the prophet, whom Old Testament scholar Walter Brueggemann calls "Israel's greatest voice of hope." Not surprising, chapters 40 to 55 in Isaiah comprise two-thirds of the Old Testament quotes cited in the New Testament. As the people of Israel linger in a foreign land and lament their losses, Isaiah asserts that God is powerfully present precisely when people feel helpless and bereft. So, here is the story.

Babylonian Captivity

The time, 588 BC. The place, Jerusalem. The Judean kingdom is in peril. Josiah, a great king who instituted reforms in the spiritual life of the Jews, has been succeeded by a line of rascals. His son Jehoiakim is unscrupulous and oppressive, a self-seeking soul schooled in luxurious living. The reforms of his father are reversed as the people put excessive trust in cultic acts to the exclusion of ethical imperatives. Jehoiachin, son of Jehoiakim, then assumes his father's throne and lasts only three months. Finally, Zedekiah, a twenty-one-year-old, takes the royal crown, but his reign of a dozen years is mired in mendacity. Arguably, he might be considered the worst of the lot. He spends his last living moments seeing his sons being killed and then having his own eyes poked out.

Josiah had destroyed pagan shrines, temples, and objects; he outlawed magic and sorcery. In reference to Josiah, Jeremiah quotes the Lord: "He defended the cause of the poor and needy, and so all went well. Is that not what it means to know me?" (Jer. 22:16). But his faithful efforts vanished in the folly of his prodigy. And now Babylon is at the city gates again, its militia preparing to assault the city. Israel was a land both blessed and threatened by its position, sitting on the major trade routes between wealthy nations. People from all corners of the known world met in Israel to trade, producing good income for the people of Israel. The trade routes that passed through their territory, however, were also the routes that military forces of the mighty powers took when they were traveling to battle to occupy each other's land. Israel had both an enviable and a vulnerable geographical location, evident in the Babylonian assault, followed by Persian, Syrian, and Roman takeovers.

Warnings had been regularly posted about the Babylonian military threat, but they were not heeded. Walter Brueggemann described the nonattentiveness as "royal deafness." With the crushing force of Nebuchadnezzar's army, Jerusalem becomes a wasteland in no time. The temple is burned, the city walls are torn down, people are slaughtered, and the streets go silent. Ten years before, the brightest and the best—the princes, the crafts-men, the priests, and the smithies—had been led to Babylon, about two hundred miles away, perhaps to render them power-less to incite any rebellion. Under Nebuchadnezzar's forces, the deportation begins again.

The Davidic throne comes to an end and with it any sem-blance of social cohesion. The Holy Land is in the hands of infidels, a sorrow of incredible proportion for the Jews. And all of this happened while the marketplace conversations and the monarch's press releases portrayed a rosy picture. Listen to Jeremiah: "They [the leaders] dress the wound of my people as though it were not serious. 'Peace, peace,' they say, when there is no peace. Are they ashamed of their loathsome con-duct? No, they have no shame at all; they do not even know how to blush" (Jer. 6:14–15). With shameless assurances, the royal word went out: "The Babylonian insurgents are in their last throes." But the prophets know the human temptation to submerge bad news. And Israel will not notice, will not respond. Leaders bury the truth and substitute pretense, saying, "Peace, peace," with a straight face rather than a blood-induced red one. Noticing the concealment, the prophet issues warnings not once or twice but repeatedly (see Jer. 20:4; 21:7; 22:24–25; 28:15–16; 36:3; 37:17).

The loss of the city, the land, the temple, and the Davidic kingship represents a tremendous shock to the Jewish people. In those days, normative Judaism meant living with the faith-ful presence of God, always accessible at the temple. Now all that is gone. Exiled from their homes, they begin to adapt to being outsiders, refugees, and distraught losers. Where was the Lord in this horrendous change of fortune? Jerusalem, temple, king—were not these the essentials of their religion and their existence as a people? How could they continue to believe they were the chosen?

The people of Zion, exiled in Babylon, found it hard to sing their songs. They hung their lyres on the willows and wept. And when the captors asked them to sing of Zion, they refused: "How shall we sing the Lord's song in a foreign land?" (Ps. 137). With their way of life upended, musical mirth would be only a form of self-mockery.

Exile and Homecoming

Things did eventually change for the Israelites. All three prophets of the exile—Isaiah, Jeremiah, and Ezekiel—spoke of "a new opportunity":

> Comfort, comfort my people, says your God. Speak tenderly to Jerusalem, and proclaim to her that her hard service has been completed, that her sin has been paid for, that she has received from the LORD's hand double for all her sins.
>
> —ISAIAH 40:1–2

> This is what the LORD says: "When seventy years are completed for Babylon, I will come to you and fulfill my gracious promise to bring you back to this place. For I know the plans I have for you," declares the LORD, "plans to prosper you and not to harm you, plans to give you hope and a future."
>
> —JEREMIAH 29:10–11

> Then he said to me: "Son of man, these bones are the whole house of Israel. They say, 'Our bones are dried up and our hope is gone; we are cut off.' . . . Say to them: . . . 'O my people, I am going to open your graves and bring you up from them; I will bring you back to the land of Israel.'"
>
> —EZEKIEL 37:11–12

God's restoration is set to begin. God has prepared a way of return. The narrative is now exile *and* homecoming, captivity *and* freedom, despair *and* hope. The prophets are the messengers of this divine process "to uproot and tear down, to destroy and overthrow, to build and to plant" (Jer. 1:10).

Dialectical Thinking

Theologians call this vital tension between opposites the dialectic of life. A dialectician is one who can hold together the truth expressed in opposites, two ideas that appear to cancel out each other. As an example, the Scripture speaks about losing your life and thereby finding it. From a biblical perspective, God's gifts and benefits can be hidden under trouble and disaster. Homecoming is hidden in exile. God establishes a straight path leading to Jerusalem after the dead-end years of captivity in Babylon. This dialectic way of thinking has deep roots in Judaism. Brueggemann cites the alternation of lament and hope as a characteristic of Jewish thought. He cites verses from the third chapter of Lamentations as an example. In verse 18, hope is gone; but then, in verse 21, hope reappears. In a broken world, hope and lament are partners. Hope does not need to silence the rumbling of crisis to be hope.[4]

Compared to an ideologue, a dialectician's thoughts are radically different. The ideologist makes no room for dialogue, for everything is reduced to here or there, this or that. There can be no ambiguity. Thus, in order to see light, the ideologist minimizes the moments of despair and erases the darkness. Ideologists oversimplify and trivialize the thick complexity of life with the authority of finality. In a gathering of ideologues, one encounters the exaggeration of the ultimacy of their answers and a neglect of disturbing questions. For an ideologue, contradictions are mentally sifted so that solutions are uncontaminated by uncertainties. "A strong ideology," theologian Kosuke Koyama

states, "cannot accept the uncertainty of brokenness."⁵ Ideology splits everything down the middle. For those who hanker
for finality and fixity—loose ends sewn together, chaos held in
check, evil assigned to those outside of our fence—exile and
homecoming is not their metaphor. But by trusting that the
God of exile can also be the God of homecoming, tension can
be engaged, not negated.

Exile and homecoming are of a piece and become the de-
cisive reference point for the self-understanding of Judaism.
And six hundred years later, the imagery becomes central to
the Christian understanding of life as death and resurrection,
being lost and found, alienated and reconciled. The paradoxical
nature of faith as exile and homecoming defines the Christian
in the world. The metaphor has cast a long shadow. Paul writes
to the Ephesians, "Consequently, you are no longer foreigners
and aliens, but fellow citizens . . ." (Eph. 2:19). And if you are
no longer in exile, abandoned to sorrow or isolated from your
hope, you can become a partner, a "fellow citizen," with God
in his new creation.

Three Temptations

The early Christians were called "the people of the way." And
they knew firsthand, as their ancestors knew, that the way always
passes through "the valley of the shadow of death" as well as
"green pastures," that, as Jesus walked the streets of Jerusalem,
the fickle crowds exchanged the chant of "Alleluia!" for outbursts
of "Crucify him!" in a matter of days. Dialectical thinking allows
one to hope in the darkness. It is easy to talk about hope when
the sun shines; but let the dark clouds of tragedy, betrayal, or
deep disappointment enter our lives, and despair hits us like a
ton of bricks. As Edwin Friedman's formula $HE = RO$ suggests,
precisely then, at the time of intense anxiety, the response of
the organism is paramount. Walter Brueggemann sees the deep

dislocations of Israel's ancient exile as foreshadowing the church's situation today.[6] The disappearance of the temple, kingship, and land are the external losses for the captives. But at a deeper level, the Israelites lost certainty, reliability, and a sense of possibility. Some of the deported Israelites accommodated to the empire's ethos, seeking safety in Babylon. Under the conditions of captivity, most had to wrestle with the temptations of denial, despair, and magic.

The same temptations can compete for the attention of today's leaders in the church. Denial is a defense against unpleasant facts and negative realities. People automatically block out information that is emotionally disturbing. Even if a greater number and weight of facts or instances support contrary information, people (individually and corporately) discount it in order to maintain the authority of their own conclusions. In physicist James Gleick's book, *Chaos: Making a New Science*, Gleick quotes Leo Tolstoy: "I know that most men, including those at ease with problems of the greatest complexity, can seldom accept even the simplest and most obvious truth if it be such as would oblige them to admit the falsity of conclusions . . . which they have proudly taught to others, and which they have woven, thread by thread, into the fabric of their lives."[7] Tolstoy's points of reference are individuals who are well trained to search for facts through observational testing. Denial is the natural working of the survival brain. Even the person trained to be objective will resort to denial in order not to be embarrassed by the negation of one's claims. Denial is the reactive brain's first line of defense. It is a buffer against shocking news.

If not denial, despair can permeate people's lives and render them helpless. *Despair* is an interesting word, as it derives from the Latin *desperare*, meaning "to give up hope." *Spes* is the Latin word for hope, as seen also in the words *desperation* and *prosperity*. But despair is a form of self-imprisonment. Despair believes in limits only. Evidences of possibility are not seen or imagined.

Locked into gloom, options are useless. For instance, Israel had forsaken its commitments to things larger than self (God, community, family), and instead turned to immediate self-absorbing things. "Why," the prophet Isaiah asked, "spend money on what is not bread, and your labor on what does not satisfy?" (55:2). Indeed, despair does not always appear as a sad face and a dour spirit. Despair can be nothing less than trusting lesser gods.

A third temptation is magic. Sorcerers have a habit of showing up in down times: "Give me your soul—and a check—and I will make it rise again." Trafficking remedies and secret formulas, these vendors promise quick and direct action. Our survival brains can be suckers for any kind of upper. James Collins, author of the best-selling business book *Good to Great: Why Some Companies Make the Leap—and Others Don't*, more recently discussed how even good and great businesses can fall. Stage three of the fall is the denial of problems. Stage four, just before failure, is grasping for saviors. As we know, the savior lineup contains many wizards. Most vulnerable to the sorcerer's secret or snake oil are the disheartened, who have their hopes scattered and their longings at a still point.

Today's Exile

The loss of members, influence, and a sense of mission—the church's misfortune of the moment—resembles the experience of Israel's exile. Congregations ask, Can we sustain our spirit? Will our corporate psyche fall to a painfully low level? Is denial, despair, or magic the best we can do?

The lesson of the present dislocation is clear, if still not learned. The era of Christendom is gone. No longer is culture subsidizing and supporting mainline churches. Now, people are both disengaging from and not affiliating with the church. Complicating matters, churches may not be influencing the lives of their members in a spiritual way. To many, religion is a good thing, as long as it provides personal comfort and meets

FIGURE **3.1.** CONTRASTING HOPEFULNESS AND HOPELESSNESS
As you glance at the columns below, where do you stand?
Where do you think your congregation may be?

HOPEFULNESS	HOPELESSNESS
Stirs imagination	Shrinks the radius of possibility
Has the capacity to wait	Becomes restless or apathetic
Sets free from preoccupation with the present hopelessness	Entraps, no way out
Expands horizons	Minimizes options
Is able to influence events	Resigns to existing conditions
Creates a sense of buoyancy	Loses heart, no spirit
References the present	Believes past has been horrible, the present is no better
Energizes	Suspends actions and decisions
Remembers the future	Is stuck in the present arrangement of things
Looks for help outside	Withdraws from interaction
Searches for a future benefit	Lives as if future is a dead end; futile thinking

individual needs. Consequently, they want the church to double the offer—to give them not only a message of salvation but also the elements of a benefits plan, such as self-improvement methods, life-coping skills, satisfaction enhancement, and stress reduction. At best, the church is viewed from a consumer's view, especially as a provider of reassurance in tough times. At worst, it is not much more than T. S. Eliot's caricature: "And the Church does not seem to be wanted / In country or in suburb; and in the town / Only for important weddings."[8]

The Church and Temptations

I have yet to work with a congregation that is in conflict or in transition, or for whatever reason paralyzed in its functioning, that moved notably beyond its present arrangement without the guidance of leaders who inspire hope in others. Remember Friedman's formula: $HE = RO$: The *hostility* of the *environment* is proportionate to the *responses* of the *organism*? Hope is a response. Hope sees the door is set open. But the same emotional phenomena troubling the Israelites besiege the church. We are dealing with denial, despair, and magic.

John Kotter's fable *Our Iceberg Is Melting* provides an illustration of denial at work. A penguin discovers the iceberg used as home by the colony may be in danger of melting. During the telling of the story, Kotter demonstrates the eight-step process of change he has discerned through his work with organizations. In the fable, Kotter introduces a character not represented in any of his steps of change but who has to be considered in the whole process. He calls him No No. By all measures, No No could be a group as well. Kotter recognizes that the eight steps are crucial for changing a system. But how to handle No No at any point in the process is incredibly significant, too. We have already examined the persistence of form (such as the firefighters running away from the flames), aided by emotional barriers and imaginative gridlock. The resistance to change is a stubborn thorn in the flesh of newness. No No personifies resistance. No No is a creature of emotionality. To get past No No, a cadre of visionaries is necessary so that hope can be a counterforce to No No's denial—"the iceberg is fine."[9]

The second temptation is despair. Despair sees a locked door and the end to any progress or financial increment. Hope, being much wiser than despair, can accept limits and be realistic. Hope will hit stubborn obstacles. But the closed door does not alone determine hope's whole field of vision. The despondent will look away; the hopeful will look around, probe, seek a way through the threshold.

As an illustration of the power of hope to bring about change, consider psychologist Herbert Lefcourt's story about an institutionalized woman who had been mute for ten years. She had to be moved from her floor, which was being remodeled, to another floor. Because of the nature of their illnesses, residents on her floor were known as "chronic-helpless." Before the patients where shuffled from unit to unit, they were given medical examinations. The mute woman's physical health was superb. After she was moved, she was able to do what patients on that new floor could do, including wander around the hospital grounds and the neighborhood streets. To the surprise of everyone, within a week of her new freedom, she began to respond to them, even speaking. Her gregariousness ended, however, when she was returned to the chronic-helpless floor. She died a week later, with no known cause of death. A world of hope was forged in a new floor, a space of openness and freedom. When she returned to the space called "chronic-helpless," the persistence of form returned with vengeance. For a week, a door had been set open. Hope emerged only to be dashed by a return of despair.[10]

Hope influences mood and behavior, which in turn affect health. In *The Anatomy of Hope: How People Prevail in the Face of Illness*, physician Jerome Groopman reports that, when a patient is feeling helpless, endorphins—natural analgesic substances produced by the body to inhibit or diminish pain—are not present. If hope can affect the physical body, what is the possibility for the body politic?

The third temptation facing churches is magic. Someone somewhere has the elixir for ailing congregations. During the exile, Jeremiah and Ezekiel warned the Israelites about a medley of enchanters. Jeremiah spoke forcefully, exhorting, "Do not listen to your prophets, your diviners, your interpreters of dreams, your mediums or your sorcerers" (Jer. 27:9). Then Ezekiel admonished the people, "Woe to the women who sew magic charms on all their wrists and make veils . . . for their heads in order to ensnare people" (Ezek. 13:18). Evidently, the soothsaying craft had enjoyed a lot of success. Unable to influence the events in their lives directly, the people of Israel turned to the enchanters, whom they thought had more power than they did. In fact, when I looked for a synonym for *magic* in my thesaurus, the third listing was the word *Chaldean*, another name for the Babylonians.

Many are drawn to magic because of its promise of quickness. Before you know it—Presto! Repeat the cant "Abracadabra." Magic is not only quick but also direct. All sorcerers go straight for the end product, without the process. Here it is. No messy stuff. No questions. No confusing dialectic to toss and turn in your brain. It seems as if every magician possesses the master key to the door.

Jesus told a story about magical thinking. A rich farmer develops what appears to be a logical business plan: "The ground of a certain rich man produced a good crop. He thought to himself, 'What shall I do? I have no place to store my crops.' Then he said, 'This is what I'll do, I will tear down my barns and build bigger ones, and there I will store all my grain and my goods.' And I'll say to myself, 'You have plenty of good things laid up for many years. Take life easy; eat, drink, and be merry.'" "The farmer is successful," Kosuke Koyama mentions, "but he is anxious."[11] And his anxiety leads him to magic—Presto! Abracadabra! Bigger barns!

I imagine a number of churches wouldn't mind having a bit of magic in their community. It might suffice for the moment, but it would also displace hope. To lose hope is to lose a valuable source for motivation. Some etymologists assert that *hope* derives from the German *hop*, which means "leaping expectations." Hope is an exuberant response, particularly when things are in reverse, in decline, and in disrepair. In the movie *Zorba the Greek*, a wealthy entrepreneur loses his profitable business and turns to his friend Zorba, and says, "Zorba, teach me to dance." In other words, "Zorba, teach me to leap, to see beyond ground zero—essentially, to hope again."

The dance metaphor for hope is central to French Catholic poet Charles Peguy's poem, "The Portal of the Mystery of Hope." He portrays the biblical idea of hope as an effervescent little girl in the Corpus Christi parade. The adults have grown tired. But the little girl (hope) is "twenty steps ahead of them." Why the exuberance?

> Hope sees what has not yet been and what will be.
> She loves what has not yet been and what will be.

In Peguy's imagery, hope "continually begins again and forever promises":

> Hope makes pure water from impure water,
> Young water from old water.
> SPRINGS FROM OLD WATER.
> Fresh souls from old souls.
> YOUNG MORNINGS FROM OLD EVENINGS.
> Clear souls from troubled souls.[12]

The source of the newness is God's grace.

Part II

The Mission

THE CHURCH EXISTS . . . for what we sometimes call "mission": to announce to the world that Jesus is its Lord. This is the "good news."

—N. T. Wright
Simply Christian

NEW CHALLENGES ARE continually arising to test the church's commitment to the mission of the gospel. When the church successfully meets a challenge, the door of history opens and the church goes forward in mission. Otherwise, the door closes and the moment of opportunity is missed. The time of opportunity for mission has never been greater than it is now.

—Carl Braaten
The Apostolic Imperative

IF THE CHURCH IS TO impart to the world a message of hope and love, of faith, justice, and peace, something of this should become visible, audible, and tangible in the church itself.

—David Bosch
Transforming Mission

CHAPTER 4

The Challenge of Change

Deep change, adaptive change, or system change—whatever one calls it—is no easy process. Change, even minor ones, can destabilize whole systems, and the homeostatic forces will take revenge. Reactivity reaches irrational highs. Polarization hardens. Seeding suspicion of others flourishes. Brazen behaviors multiply. Blaming metastasizes like cancer. Anne Lamott, who has written both fiction and nonfiction, and more recently on faith, sagely advises, "So when the seasons change, buckle up."[1]

With a similar viewpoint, Edwin Friedman discusses change and leadership: "Not only are we entering a millennium of perpetual novelty but also the future promises a continuous escalation in the rate of change. This change will have a significant effect on the emotional processes of all families and other institutions."[2] Friedman foresaw these circumstances perpetuating a chronically anxious state for the most immature members of society and creating a condition of permanent stress for all leaders.[3] How will the church find leaders for emotional systems caught in a rising tide of change?

Where's Charlie?

Sitting on a park bench, a man observed a couple of workmen. At first he was baffled, but soon became amused. He thought

49

to himself, "Am I seeing what I'm seeing?" One worker would take his shovel and dig a hole two to three feet deep. The second workman would use his shovel to return the dirt into the hole. After watching them do this digging ritual, the man left the bench and approached the two workmen. "May I ask what you are doing? I'm curious." The first worker said that they were planting trees. "I dig the hole," he stated, "and Charlie puts the plant in the hole, and Chester here fills the hole with dirt. Charlie is out sick today."

Tree planting goes on the same way with or without Charlie. As facetious as the story is, it still portrays the sheer difficulty of changing what is emotionally encrusted. We see change rebuffed even when it produces vitality or improvements. Marius von Senden's book *Space and Sight* is about the dramatic change in the lives of people who underwent the first successful cataract surgeries. Blind from birth, they receive the sudden and wondrous gifts of sight, but their experiences are not all positive. Von Senden collected accounts of their postsurgery experiences. He discovered that the patients had no sense of space. They had no idea of form, size, and distance. When a doctor asked one of the patients to show him how big her mother was, she held her two index fingers only a few inches apart. A second patient, looking at photographs and paintings, asked why someone had put dark marks all over them. "Those aren't dark marks," the mother of the nearsighted girl explained, "those are shadows. It is one of the ways the eye knows that things have shape. If it were not for shadows, many things would look flat." The daughter responded: "Well, that's how things do look. Everything looks flat with dark patches."[4]

The effort to see in a new way proved overwhelming for other patients. They found tremendous size to be disturbing in comparison to what they previously conceived of as something manageable by touch. Realizing for the first time they were visible to others, they felt uncomfortable. Seeing themselves in

a mirror was a bewildering experience. The father of a young adult who had hoped for so much from this operation expressed perplexity, noting that his daughter would shut her eyes to go about the house, especially when she approached a staircase. He wrote that "she is never happier or more at ease than when, by closing her eyelids, she relapses into her former state of total blindness." Tormented by his experience of new sight, a teenage boy blurted out, "If things aren't altered, I'll tear my eyes out." Still, some learned to see in a new way. One patient exclaimed repeatedly, "Oh, God, how beautiful."[5]

Tear out their eyes? Go blind at a staircase? Imprisoned in darkness, liberated by light, surrounded by the wonder of color and depth—and yet, <u>many newly sighted people wanted to return to what was known and familiar</u>. Even in the face of this marvelous sensory improvement, the forces of sameness were potent.

Change and Emotionality

Change will not advance very far or last very long if the challenge of change is not understood and handled adequately. <u>Change</u>

will touch off a burst of emotional energy. I have experienced it myself in working with congregations. Occasionally, I may be surprised by the vehemence or the source of the emotionality, but never its presence. Congregations ask me to help them move out of a mess, morass, or maze. The process I use eventually produces proposals for change. But someone or some group will grind their emotional axe in order to hatchet the process. If the change is not what they expect, they try to cut off its legs. After he coauthored *Reengineering the Corporation*, based on his engineering background, Michael Hammer admitted that 65 to 75 percent of companies that used his formula for restructuring businesses failed because they insufficiently appreciated the human dimension.[6] If you are going to consider the human side of things, Hammer insists, you will attend to emotional dynamics.

Economists George Akerlof and Robert Shiller underscore Hammer's insight. In economic theory, they observed that a disproportionate emphasis had been placed on rational behavior to the undervaluing of irrational, misguided behaviors in financial decision making. More consideration, the two claim, needed to be given to the inconsistent, restless elements in the economy—powerful psychological forces that they refer to as "animal spirits." People, it had been assumed, would decide solely on the basis of enlightened self-interest to generate wealth. But animal spirits, the primitive urge to action, plays a significant part in financial choices. Our economic behavior is not fully rational. In monetary matters, people's level of confidence, illusions about money, and beliefs about fairness can never be disregarded. To illustrate their point, Akerlof and Shiller talk about a game that experimenters devised for basic sharing among people. By acting cooperatively, the players ensured profitable returns for the whole group. However, the experimenters offered players an incentive to perform for self-interest. The researchers discerned that, with each round, if some players detected that other players were playing selfishly, they would defect too. With many repetitions of the game, all the people succumbed to self-interest. In essence, the emotional forces trumped rational ones.[7]

People in the church can make the same wrong assumptions as some economists; we can believe that, in a church community, people will behave rationally, thereby extending goodwill, patience, and respect when interacting with others. We think our core values, like cream, will rise to the top. We think that if we make a few sensible changes, harmony will hold. But animal spirits find their way into any system.

Change in Steps

I witnessed an example of animal spirits in a congregation where a clergyperson thought revitalization of the parish was at his fingertips. Without any consultation, he quickly made changes. After the previous pastor's twenty-six-year stint, a contingency of the congregation yearned for something new. Bolstered by the new senior pastor's bold innovations, they immediately aligned themselves with him. Actually, the trouble started when he unilaterally changed the times, the style, and the leaders of the worship services. Besides changes in worship, the senior pastor rearranged the church staff, much to the dismay of the staff and their lay partners. Again, he juggled the positions without collaboration. A sizeable segment of the three thousand members became emotionally ruffled when he wrote a newsletter article telling them he was not going to "hold your hands" and be "an enabler of your dependencies." But his supporters liked his command-and-control leadership, especially after the plodding two-and-a-half decades of the "Reverend Right Friendly." But allies of the former pastor were not about to let "Dr. Change-love," as they called him, disrupt familiar patterns.

The acrimonious conflict became so inflamed that friends and relatives ceased talking to one another. Each group stood emotionally riveted to its own side of the controversy. Then, suddenly, the senior pastor resigned, and he also disappeared for three weeks. When he returned, he learned that no action had been taken on his resignation, and he sought to retract it. When the leaders announced that he would preach on the following Sunday, the opposition turned their sour complaints into acid threats. A couple of brothers who owned a business together but stood on the opposite sides of the matter convinced the leaders to delay his return to the pulpit for the moment, until the resignation matter was settled. After he had been prohibited to preach, he abruptly scorched a few of his own supporters publicly for being cowardly and "maintenance mongers," acquiescing as they did to the request that he not preach. In contrast, his militant sponsors were invited to his house for a cookout. But the bitterness grew. Unannounced, he left a second time, but with his wife, child, and furnishings. Some were pleased, but his strong base of support only became much more committed to him. Some stayed in touch with him, pleading with him to return.

On my first visit to the congregation, a professor from a local university told me that, in her view, the senior pastor was a "change missionary" who failed to mobilize "the change agents" to deal with "the culture keepers." Her comment reminded me of John Kotter's wisdom regarding the change process. John Kotter is professor emeritus of Harvard University, and based on his study of the change process, he has established a series of eight steps for making significant change, requiring a considerable length of time. Not surprising, Kotter states that "an appalling 70 percent of the companies" he watched initiate change miscarried in the very first phase. Contributors to the early failures, he notes, are people with little experience in renewing organizations; the strain of moving people out of their comfort zones; the trendsetters' lack of patience; and leaders sharing too little information about the vision to others, overcomplicating the vision, neglecting to plan early-term celebrations to maintain a sense of urgency, and losing subsequent nerve. As you glance at his eight stages noted in figure 4.1, keep in mind that there

FIGURE 4.1. Eɪɢʜᴛ Sᴛᴇᴘs ᴛᴏ Sɪɢɴɪꜰɪᴄᴀɴᴛ Cʜᴀɴɢᴇ (adapted from John Kotter)[8]

STEPS	NEEDED ACTION	DANGER SIGNS
1. Establish a sense of urgency (motivate, *carpe diem*).	Describe the realities as both potential crisis and a new opportunity.	Being highly anxious about disturbing the emotional system; risk-avoidant behavior (delaying decisions, not responding to early criticism)
2. Form strong guiding coalition (identify leaders to guide process).	Assemble a group of mature, motivated people committed to the change effort.	Not recognizing how difficult it is to move people out of their comfort zones, and most people are late adopters of change
3. Create a vision (present a picture of the future).	Use the vision and its images to mobilize people's energy; images stir up hope; people respond.	Giving halfhearted support, or no support
4. Communicate the vision (clarify who we are, what we are about).	Encourage and enlist others in contributing ideas and activities.	Presenting a vision that is too grandiose, too nebulous, or too complicated
5. Empower others to act on the vision (create a network of influence).	Share the vision widely, clearly, dramatically.	Allowing resisters to sabotage the change effort through their threats
6. Consolidate change and plan for more (build on imagination).	Emotionally recharge the process with freshness, using rituals for marker events, offering praise for achievements.	Assuming vision is known and accepted
7. Incorporate new approaches into the system (affirm "This is our way").	Keep momentum going by affirming what has happened.	Lagging zeal, letting routine "run" the process; declaring victory too soon
8. Identify and train new leaders to continue what has been started (make a commitment to the future).	Introduce new leaders to sustain and oversee the change process.	Not staying with the process; not having leaders ready; mission drift

are no shortcuts. It all has to start with urgency, not with good intentions, panicky decisions, or mere preferences. Likewise, Kotter himself reminds his readers of the "powerful role that emotions played" in this process.[9]

Clergy and Change

In twenty-seven of my last thirty-three interventions with congregations, battle lines were drawn relative to a particular change or to the process of change itself. In general, "significant change" is not a preferred future for congregations. I have not found much aptitude in clergy to guide such a change or much urgency among lay leaders to initiate it. More often, the leaders are expected to stay inside the box of day-to-day problems. Changes that might adjust the design or balance of the system are not pressing priorities. <u>Many congregations take pride in their homeostatic ways</u>.

Further, many clergy are caught in a vise, having been trained to be priestly in their ministry but having received little assistance in being prophetic and visionary. The priest is the consoler, the reconciler, and the soul friend. Relational abilities are paramount. Healing is the centerpiece of this activity. The prophet is one who speaks out, who is a truth teller, though not brash or cynical, for the prophet cares about people but at times may use militant words. Awareness and action are the heart of the prophet's work. The visionary role includes governance, oversight, and planning. Vision is the key to this ministry. Since about 80 percent of churches in the United States have two hundred members or fewer, the more relational role of priest remains the most prominent for clergy. The need for comfort is ongoing.

Now, suddenly, with steep changes happening in our society, congregations have to ask themselves whether they are responding to a world that no longer exists and whether they have the sort of leadership required to shift to new understanding and practices. Surely, the priestly work is always needed, but now, especially now, clergy may need to become advocates for adaptive change. Ask yourselves—does your congregation need a more prophetic ministry? Do you need a more visionary type of ministry? My experience indicates that many congregations would opt for the priestly role: If we just had a pastor who loved us, we would be all right. Other congregations would not contest that, but would want the love to be engaged with justice, mission, and new visions. Certainly, Kotter's first step—establishing a sense of urgency—is more akin to prophetic efforts, to creating a vision. Laity who understand today's new world are asking clergy to do more than preach the gospel and administer the sacraments. At their moment of dislocation, they are requesting a leader to help them become and stay focused.

What is needed in today's world, awareness and vision, may not be the gift a particular clergyperson can offer. While scores of books, workshops, and seminars are devoted to transformational leadership, those who work closely with churches and clergy realize that clergy are not well prepared to institute change on a system level. Training is being offered clergy with the hope that they will learn to function in the new context by embracing (1) the reality that arduous effort is needed to move an emotional system to a new way of seeing itself and a novel way of responding to its context; (2) the work of transformation by offering knowledge of the change process and the need for emotional stamina to stay the course; and (3) the importance of connecting change with mission.

Transformation Magic

I have my doubts about much of the transformational leadership training being offered. Most of it is about implementing a pattern developed elsewhere and has to do with technique and data collection. This is unfortunate. To give you an illustration: I received an advertisement from a church consulting group promising potential participants a transformed church. Eight churches they worked with attested to their success. The brochure had the appeal of magic—quick and direct. I have no doubt changes occurred. But congregations needing change are not congregations automatically ready for change. What is missing in the ad, and in a lot of training efforts, are the failures. Some churches didn't make it. What didn't work, and with whom? I would like to see a transformation project that says, "Let us prepare your congregation for change. Buckle up!"

However, no reference is made to the periodic regression that will happen. The promotional material treats transformation as if it were an event, not an ongoing process. I paraphrase what is contained in the promotional piece:

> *Back Then:* "We were satisfied with what we had and what we did. Our needs were met. We were a community of people with the purpose of serving ourselves. Well intentioned, nonetheless, we were off course."

> *Right Now:* "We are empowered disciples. We have weaned ourselves from programs and organizational trivia. We are focused on making a difference. Instead of going from outside to inside, we go from inside to outside."

The turnaround is presented as a completed process. Misfirings and mistakes, bumps and rubs, losses and defections, turmoil and tears—none are reported. From "Back Then" to "Right Now" is practically effortless. The change process is depicted as linear, with the same results for everyone. I am obviously overdrawing the point, but I see too many congregations that want what the promotional material promises—swift and simple change, little tension, rare confusion, and a normal range of emotionality. Even Michael Hammer and John Kotter admit that only one out of four organizations they worked with made significant change.

Despite my doubts, I appreciate the transformational leadership movement. As Friedman announced, a world of "perpetual novelty" is creating a situation of "permanent stress" for all leaders. All help is welcome. But my stream of doubt about the transformation training efforts is still flowing. I openly admit my bias. Fear goes off on its own course, regardless of anyone's ironclad process. Change, like someone saying the word *cancer*, makes a direct hit at the amygdala. To make transformation appear easy and rosy is to miss entirely the power of emotional forces. I have seen clergy thrown to the antichange wolves. An excited clergyperson full of energy and ideas is no guarantee that modifications are only months away. I have witnessed self-declared transformational leaders butting their heads against emotional barriers. As an interventionist with conflicted churches, I have my own bruises and wounds from efforts at change. Congregations even hire me for that purpose, to move them out of their systemic paralysis, and yet some cannot muster the courage or imagination to break the gridlock. Since the churches are remunerating me for my services, one would assume they would be ready to move beyond their anxiety-generated immobility. But saying, "We want to change," and actually changing are entirely different matters. Transformation redefines who we are and what we do. It is always an emotional experience. For one thing, transformation begins with *endings*. Death comes to the system in some form. The natural response is for people to grieve. As Ronald Heifetz notes in *Leadership on the Line*, leaders become vulnerable to people's grievances. Action tends to cease or slow down when grievances are strong. Grieving has a way of putting us on hold before it gently lets us go.

Transformation is a process. It may take five years, a generation, or perhaps even forty wilderness years to see its effects. Early in the process it isn't possible to tell how transformed a church might become. So impatient and anxious, well-intended change agents turn a decade into an hour.

Who Are We?

Today's renewal efforts have a jargon. The terms *comeback*, *revitalized, turnaround,* and *redeveloped churches* have become familiar. In another time, churches placed in these classifications pioneered growth, but now they are coping with change as their numbers plummet or gradually decline. Congregations that may have had 1,000 members in 1985 have fewer than 200 today; congregations with 800 members only ten years ago have had to face a 30 percent drop to 480 members. The success rate for a turnaround church is reported to be no better than what Kotter reported for businesses—about one in four. People can squelch urgency by dragging out possible negative results and impending doom. If leaders want to implement change, they are placed under suspicion. With fear hovering in the community, the coalition of change agents that needs to develop doesn't know how to get started, or they prefer add-ons rather than substantive changes.

The challenge of change for a congregation on a steady downward slope is precisely to redefine and redirect its mission. They have to realize that a decline in growth is not an end to mission. Yes, they are mere shadows of their past. Yes, rethinking mission is difficult, for congregations are burdened by big or deteriorating buildings, smaller staffs, a paucity of young families, and a shortage of hope. But expansion is not the sole gauge of mission orientation. One problem with this thinking is the belief that, for congregations, all things are equal. But congregations are not in the same place, same stage, or same circumstance. That's not reality. Best-selling author Kathleen Norris talks about her old Presbyterian congregation, Hope Church, in Hope, South Dakota. Both the community of Hope and Hope Church are paradoxes. Although dying, they are, in Norris's words, "beautifully alive." The vitality is a result of an unflinching refusal to despair. Due to population depletion, the continuous flight of youth to urban areas, and the sheer isolation geographically, numerical growth is not possible. Despair? According to Norris, the people refuse its presence. The congregation actively participates in reducing world hunger and ranks high in percentage giving among Presbyterians in South Dakota. "The power of Hope Church and country churches like it is subtle and not easily quantifiable. It's a power derived from smallness and lack of power, a concept the apostle Paul would appreciate, even if modern church bureaucrats lose sight of it. Their challenge is to go on living thankfully, contributing liberally, and living graciously."[10] Quality can be a measure of mission, too. Many churches like Hope will not grow. Some are hospice cases. But, not one of them is outside the realm of mission. I want to underscore that growth, as significant as it is for mission, does not alone define what mission is. To assign "mission" as a title exclusively to numerically growing churches is a mistaken understanding of mission.

In his classic study, *Transforming Mission*, missiologist David Bosch reported that the Bible passage called the Great Commission, Matthew 28:18–20, was not understood to be primarily about mission until the early nineteenth century. Before then, the verses were read as part of the rite of baptism. Biblical scholarship has revealed that the mandate "Go!" is not in the original Greek. It is a participle—"going." The translation would be "as you go." Mennonite theologian David Augsburger notes how broad the mission is with this simple change of "as you go": "As you live, as you go about your daily work, as you move to new settings for service, as you join or create new communities of discipleship, as you fulfill your vocation as a follower of Jesus— you shall be witnesses. This is not a sales strategy. This is not a mandate for mass media. This is not a justification for a state-church takeover of a people's religious affiliation. This is not a method for achieving church growth. This is a call to authentic, faithful witness in all of life."[11] Whether you are a member of

Hope Church in Hope, South Dakota, or a megachurch in an urban setting, you can be a witness to the gospel in all of life. Maybe that's the way to transform your church.

CHAPTER 5

The Making of a Mission Culture

*V*isiting a relative who lives on the Great South Bay off the shores of Long Island, several of us joined him for a boat ride. We were on the bay in early afternoon, enjoying the breeze and fast ride. Some dark, scattered clouds cast shadows on the water, but the sky was mostly blue. The weather forecast called for sunshine with scattered showers in the evening. But several of the dark clouds suddenly bonded together. A strong breeze accompanied the darkening sky. Within minutes, everything became gray, concealing any sight of land. The wind-driven rain made visibility even more difficult. Unable to see land, the skipper turned to his boat's compass to orient himself and the boat. Motoring slowly, he was able to dodge other boats on the bay as we headed for the now-invisible shore. Eventually, we saw partial outlines of beach houses as we approached land. Totally drenched and hyperalert on our own adrenaline, we docked at our destination. Oriented by the boat's compass, we escaped harm's way, landing safely.

Toward an End

To be headed in a direction serves people well in life, just as it did for us on the bay. According to Edwin Friedman, a distinctive mark of a mature person is having clear life goals. Guided by personal goals, an individual is less likely to be distracted or detoured by the reactivity of others. Someone else's behavior does not determine yours. Based on principles and values, you direct your life. Friedman often referred to the analogy of sailing to illustrate his point. Without a destination, a sailor on a lake meanders and drifts. The sailor will not adjust the sails to take advantage of the wind to proceed to the chosen landing place. If this is true on water, what about in life? Is orientation possible without destination?

In the view of psychologist William Sheldon, having a direction is a deep, psychic need: "Continuing observation in clinical practice led almost inevitably to the conclusion that deeper and more fundamental than sexuality, deeper than the craving for social power, deeper than the desire for possessions, there is a still more generalized and universal craving in the human makeup. It is the craving for knowledge of the right direction—for orientation."[1] Sheldon's contention is that having a clear path forward is basic to life. At the biological level, the same teleological functioning is seen in bacteria. Bacteria swim for a living. If their flagella turn counterclockwise, they swim in a straight path. If, however, the flagella turn clockwise, bacteria change direction erratically. They tumble. What determines whether the flagella swim directly or erratically? If the scent of food is weak, the bacteria tumble; if the scent is stronger, they orient themselves toward the food source. Eventually, they find food, despite some erratic tumbles. When the scent is strong, bacteria move directly to enjoy a meal.

I encountered Sheldon's universal craving with two friends, both of whom had recently become widowers. Mourning the deaths of their spouses, they spoke of how *out of place* they felt, even in settings that formerly were familiar. One said, "I don't know where I fit or belong." Questions about restructuring their futures seemed overwhelming. "I'm stuck in the loss column," the second friend stated, "and I don't have much energy to move beyond it." Their deep personal losses left them disoriented. They were in the tumbling stage.

A sense of direction is just as necessary for groups of people as it is for individuals. David Brooks, op-ed writer for the *New York Times*, posed a hypothesis in a column called "The Power of Posterity." What would happen if a freakish accident involving the sun sterilized half of the population of the earth? Brooks muses. He posits that after the initial shock, people would go on with their lives in a normal way. Many people, although unable to reproduce, have lived productive, happy lives. But fifteen to twenty years after the disaster, Brooks foresees major consequences. A brutal competition between those who can produce offspring and those who cannot would erupt. Without the hope of posterity, one group could easily obsess on the here and now. Meanwhile, the other group would prepare for future gain. Here and now, the nonposterity group, Brooks assumes, would be more likely to spend rather than save money, affecting prices and economic balance. Without posterity, religion would suffer immeasurably. "Both Judaism and Christianity," Brooks notes, "are promise-centered faiths." Both have narratives centered in expectation and hope. A creeping sense of forsakenness would undermine meaning and purpose. Life would be relegated to the present, and hope would be superfluous. Some would have no interest in medical research, educational reform, or any long-term project. People simply would not recall how they rely on the "invisible and unacknowledged force" of the unborn to draw us forward. Posterity is a gift of life. Life moves towards life.[2]

Mission Drift

Considering all of the complexities and challenges facing churches, it is amazing that more of them are not on the brink of oblivion or in harm's way. Many are not using a compass to navigate the hazy conditions created by cultural shift. When consulting with churches embroiled in conflict or paralyzed by passivity, I always ask the congregation, "Does this congregation have a clear sense of its mission?" Typical responses range from "poor sense of purpose" to "running in circles," from "lack of vision" to "our mission is not to have a mission." Questions like, Who are we? What is our primary focus? go begging for answers. Then when I ask individuals what they think the mission is, the answers are rote: "spread the word," "support the church," "love everyone," and "preach the Bible." No one has ever said, "Our mission is to turn the world upside-down," or "to join God's ongoing promise to recreate the world," or "to let the world know that the resurrection means the world has not seen the last of Jesus Christ." Some members believed their congregation had a sense of mission because they had a mission statement. Sad to say, few knew what it was.

Limping along without a focus is called *mission drift*. It is what happens when people come together to support an objective but forget what the objective is. People lose their reason for being, even though they go through the motions. Many things contribute to the sidetracking, such as compromising ideals in succumbing to a pressure group, searching for instant viability or solutions, grasping for saviors, fooling themselves that they are vital or viable simply because they endure, preoccupying themselves with nonessentials, exchanging their core beliefs for more marketable ideas, or failing to attend to what God is calling them to do in their little corner of the world.

A simple example of mission drift is seen in the way U.S. citizens follow through or make good on the Pledge of Allegiance. People boldly recite the words "with liberty and justice for all." But who loses sleep at night because reality lags behind this basic principle? Or is it the other way around? Who sets their sails in the daytime to work in behalf of the lofty enterprise?

Based on my experience, congregations in mission drift will at some point:

- engage in conflict,
- suffer a malaise of spirit,
- decline in some statistical manner,
- adapt to their most immature members,
- fail to mobilize people's gifts and energy,
- surrender to apathy or complacency,
- do little planning,
- become turned in on themselves,
- blame outside forces (perhaps one another) for their depression,
- be unable to make effective, appropriate changes.

Mission Meaning

If mission is so essential to the congregation's life and well-being, what exactly does *mission* mean? In the past, the word has been used in such a way that its meaning has been distorted. For instance, when I left seminary, I was assigned to be a *missionary at large*. What this meant was I had been given the task to start a new congregation in a small town in Virginia. Once the congregation began to form, it was called a *mission congregation*. Often, congregations that are financially dependent and small are labeled in this manner. We were supported by *mission funds* given by other congregations. From these uses of the word, one can conclude that *mission* indicates something new and not self-supporting. After four years, we became a full-fledged congregation (able to support ourselves). I was no longer designated a missionary at large, and the congregation lost its title as a mission.

This misuse of the word *mission* continues today. There is a movement called "the missional church." People assign marks or attribute certain actions to a missional church. One source uses code phrases, such as "from texting to sending," "from decision to disciple," "from organization to organism," and "from demographics to discernment." I am not sure people understand the meaning of it all. In addition, I find the use of the term *missional church* confusing. It is similar to saying "the ruling government" or the "athleticism of the athlete." Either a church is missional or it is not the church. *Mission is the nature and purpose of the church*, not some list of qualifiers.

Because God has a mission, a church arises. Apart from mission, the church is meaningless. The mission has churches. Seminary professor Craig Van Gelder notes, "The church does what it is."[3] In 1952, at a conference held by the International Missionary Council, a new phrase came into use—*missio dei*. Essentially, it means mission belongs to God. The church's mission is not its own. A number of people have claimed that mission is an attribute of God. God the Father sends the Son; the Son sends the Spirit; and Father, Son, and Spirit send the church into the world.

The Latin word *missio* means "sending." The English language has words derived from *missio*, indicating movement: dismissal (departure); admission (entrance); promise (send before); submission (go under); and missile (fired object). Every baptized person is called to be a disciple responsible for taking action in behalf of God's multifaceted mission. Missiologist David Bosch writes, "Mission is the church sent into the world to love, to serve, to preach, to teach, to heal, to liberate."[4] In his study of the images of the church in the New Testament, theologian Paul Minear examines ninety words by which first-century Christian congregations articulated their sense of who they were and what they did. Most of the images are about *outward activity*, including light, salt, vine, and leaven. Each of these elements completes itself by expanding itself: Light provides warmth and enhances vision, salt preserves other foods, a vine carries nutrients to a

cluster of grapes, and leaven expands the dough.[5] Surely the church's destination is forward, reaching beyond any borders and touching every aspect of life.

An additional confusion about the word *mission* comes from assuming mission necessarily results in growth. Distinguishing between congregations in survival mode (not growing) and those in mission (growing) is not honest and certainly not helpful. Every congregation, as a living system, is in the survival business. Thousands of congregations are decreasing in numbers, but some are also alive and sensitive to mission. Who is to condemn them to the category of survival? In addition, growth is not a value in itself. It is a process. Cancer is a disease of cells that lack the capacity to stop growing. It destroys life. Growth can indicate maturing as well as increasing in metrics. Lesslie Newbigin, respected missiologist, notes that in the New Testament, joy surrounds the rapid growth in the early days of the church, yet no evidence supports that numerical growth is an ultimate concern. All things eventually reach their maximum growth. Are they then to be renamed as survival systems?

Survival is fundamental to all organic life. Anything can be eliminated, obliterated, or cremated. Survival is not the church's problem. The threat of it may even be the very stimulus needed for new action and direction. In *Christianity for the Rest of Us*, church historian Diana Butler Bass notes that the congregations she studied made changes because of normal decline, financial crisis, or neighborhood transition. Issues of survival challenged them to examine their self-understanding as people of God, asking themselves, Who are we? What is God calling us to be?

If the word *mission* is attributed only to congregations increasing in numbers, the three congregations described below would have to be omitted from the list. They are in numerical decline (see figures 5.1, 5.2, and 5.3). But they are self-consciously and intentionally working on sustaining their mission orientation. Indeed, they have spiritual spunk. They have been searching for ways to pass through the door set open.

Congregation A (Pennsylvania) is about eighty years old. It has modest facilities and a central location but a demographic dilemma. The old pattern of children and grandchildren following in the denominational footprints of their parents has practically ended. Besides, the economy in the area cannot offer enough jobs for youth who are entering the work world. Farm life is no longer a matter of generational hand-me-downs. The old industries have either moved to new locations or no longer exist. Population in the county reflects these trends, though the decrease has slowed as the area repositions its economy. A unique feature of this particular part of the state is the high population of citizens who have served in the military, including members of this congregation. They have seen other parts of the world, have embraced service as part of their identity, and have benefited from their education within the military.

A glance at Congregation A's statistics reveals the downturn both in membership and worship attendance. Yet, as the numbers ebb, overall giving is increasing. Funds designated for "mission" have tripled in ten years, although one would have expected the congregation to suffer from a severe financial shortage. Perhaps more amazing is the increase from 10 percent to 33 percent of the budget for the category of mission. When I inquired about these statistics, the majority attributed them to

FIGURE 5.1. CONGREGATION A (PENNSYLVANIA)

YEAR	MEMBERSHIP	ATTENDANCE	BUDGET	ACTUAL EXPENSES (in thousands of dollars)	MISSION EXPENSES (as part of total exp.)
1992	600	345	228	262	73
1993	623	352	232	230	69
1994	630	358	246	251	81
1995	617	311	249	230	75
1996	550	339	295	286	93
1997	559	331	325	321	107
1998	559	328	353	382	138
1999	552	324	380	381	137
2000	507	315	418	413	149
2001	497	301	474	544	211
2002	503	289	546	488	178
2003	454	280	559	467	154
2004	457	272	499	488	158
2005	430	265	529	508	147
2006	421	254	563	555	173
2007	414	230	578	513	165
2008	412	227	540	542	172

the new pastor who came in 1996 and his emphasis on stewardship. He recruited a number of the ex-military members to work alongside him. The pastor also encouraged mission trips, planned Bible studies to lift the people's vision, and devoted time to lay leadership training.

Congregation B (California) would not fit the label "mission" if numbers were the gauge. Its golden age extended from 1954 to 1964. Then, for a dozen years, a downward trend occurred before worship attendance became steady. The congregation is located in an "old" suburb, the first ring of towns circling the city. Now, the "new" suburbs lie three to four towns deep beyond

FIGURE 5.2. CONGREGATION B (CALIFORNIA)
WORSHIP ATTENDANCE 1952–2008

1952	208	1960	252	1970	256	1980	210	1990	180	2000	120
1954	195	1962	244	1972	255	1982	149	1992	162	2002	105
1956	215	1964	249	1974	243	1984	192	1994	152	2004	119
1958	230	1966	252	1976	235	1986	198	1996	136	2006	112
		1968	256	1978	222	1988	171	1998	127	2008	109

the city line. The homes in the old suburb are small, occupied by young or older couples. In fact, the neighborhood school has closed because the young families are smaller in comparison to the first settlers. Half of Congregation B's members drive more than ten miles to worship there—a pattern repeated in neighboring churches. What makes Congregation B special is its proactive laity. Sensing a need to challenge the congregation, the pastor and the parish nurse collaborated in designing what they called a holistic approach to ministry. So, for instance, they had the congregation develop a stewardship plan that expanded pledging beyond money. The members were asked to pledge a personal mission gift to the community. Some started a food pantry; some started a "Walk for Wheels," using donations to purchase wheelchairs for needy people in poor countries. Because of the number of elderly in the neighborhood, ministries were formed to provide special assistance for them.

Congregation C (Ohio) reflects the same pattern of losses as the first two congregations. In eighteen years, membership has declined from 1,200 to 541. Worship attendance mirrored the same percentage of loss. Of the three congregations, Congregation C has had the most internal problems: an assistant pastor involved in sexual misconduct, a couple of lay leaders convicted and sentenced for fraud, and a pastor's health problems necessitating his resignation and polarizing the membership. The

FIGURE 5.3. CONGREGATION C (OHIO)

Year	Total Members	Average Attendance
1990	1181	510
1991	1169	503
1992	1113	456
1993	1077	357
1994	1026	352
1995	877	326
1996	819	300
1997	844	312
1998	798	300
1999	758	320
2000	655	292
2001	632	293
2002	625	286
2003	630	275
2004	594	270
2005	578	252
2006	557	250
2007	554	248
2008	541	249

congregation had four retired pastors among its members. Two of them, a former missionary and a prison chaplain, initiated several projects. The congregation distributed Bibles to new migrants in the community and provided useful information and counsel to them. They planted a congregation in a prison unit. The youth caught a sense of urgency for mission and served lunches after worship once a month. The proceeds were used to pay the school tuition for a nine-year-old boy in their church school whose mother's bout with cancer limited her ability to pay the tuition.

The response of the three congregations to individuals and their communities may be exceptional. In similar circumstances, other congregations might still have one foot in Christendom, waiting for people to show up at their doorstep and sign on as members. Other churches continue to expect the pastor to be exclusively a chaplain (priest) who services their needs and preferences with an occasional nod to the world outside the congregation. And countless churches are still floundering, trying to understand why they exist. Mission drift is especially problematical for those churches that have experienced a steady decline in membership. A church that once numbered one thousand and now is supported by two hundred is a significantly different church. The *mission* is the same, but the refocusing needed for directing it escapes their imagination. Further, systems theory refers to an individual's functioning position, a specific way of behaving. Organizations, like people, are emotional systems that also develop ways of functioning. As congregations decline, their functioning position changes, yet many continue to function as if nothing has changed. For example, a congregation with a dwindling membership has a long tradition of having two pastors, but now two may be a luxury, perhaps a financial burden, and it has to learn to function with one pastor.

Numbers change. People represented by these numbers change. The context in which congregations find themselves changes. But the mission is what it is all about.

A Mission Primer

The church stands in service of God's love for the world. Mission begins with "God so loved *the world*," not simply those who show interest in him. Mission is about God turning toward the world in Christ. Mission is because God is a God of promise (*promissio*). God is trustworthy. God's mission of love results in the defeat of death, the transformation of lives, and the renewal of the whole creation. The church is "called, gathered, and enlightened," writes Martin Luther, to give witness to God's generosity and generativity. The mission of God embraces both the words and the works of love. The mission of God is about justification of the sinner and justice for all people; it is about a message of redemption and a mandate to attend to the poor. For a couple of centuries, the North American church distinguished between witnessing, which was considered essential, and acts of mercy, which were optional. But missionaries returning from foreign lands reminded the North American church that the talk in absence of the walk neither held people's attention nor secured their commitment. And biblical scholars noted that Jesus preached the good news *and* healed the sick. Both are signs of the kingdom of God. Giving instructions to his disciples, Jesus says, "As you go, preach this message: 'The kingdom of [God] is near.' Heal the sick, raise the dead, cleanse those who have leprosy, drive out demons" (Matt. 10:7, 8). Unfortunately, the sending instructions have received more lip service than flesh-and-blood action.

I learned a number of things working with churches, and I listed them in the introduction. Several—such as effective leaders, working a plan from the ground up, making changes for the sake of mission, and grounding efforts in theology—are obvious in Congregations A, B, and C. I didn't elaborate on the messiness that erupted when changes were implemented, although, as one can imagine, that happened too.

"If the gospel isn't transforming you," N. T. Wright asks, "how do you know that it will transform anything else?"[6] People who work for a clear mission in the church and for the wider world need to be experiencing transformation in their own lives. The following is a paraphrase of what one person in Congregation A told me about her own transformation:

> I am richly loved, a love as unprecedented and incredible as it is unconditional and undeserved. In turn, my love of God, as imperfect

and partial as it may be, moves me to want to be a part of God's mission. To lock myself into a self-absorbing spirituality is to make me the purpose of it all. But Easter is the opening chapter of the world's rebirth. You quoted Bishop Wright, saying, Easter is the big bang of new creation, that it is God's transformation of heaven and earth. My hope embraces plants, planets, and people. God's renewal begins with myself, and goes beyond the stars.

Her magnificent confession led her to believe that life is a small opportunity to live and serve God.

If you are interested in shaping and informing a mission culture in your congregation, reflect on British bishop and New Testament scholar N. T. Wright's affirmation:

> What I am saying is, think through the hope that is ours in the gospel; recognize the renewal of creation as both the goal of all things in Christ and the achievement that has already been accomplished in the resurrection; and go to the work of justice, beauty, evangelism, the renewal of space, time, and matter as the anticipation of the eventual goal and the implementation of what Jesus achieved in his death and resurrection. That is the way both to the genuine mission of God and to the shaping of the church by and for that mission.[7]

Leaders Focus on Mission

All forms of matter organize into relationships. A natural, pervasive search for connections exists. When people or things come together, it is to accomplish more, to create something new, and to discover fresh possibilities. Life seeks to organize so that more life can flourish. When we remember why we have come together, we participate in this phenomenon of expanding and deepening life. The human body is a coming together of many cells. Each cell functions in a particular way to maintain the health of the organism. Cells influence one another. Mutual interactions between cells are always occurring. They work together through a multiple, interwoven signaling system for the benefit of the whole body. Multicellular organisms have significant advantages. They are capable of greater responsiveness and adaptability. The human body, composed of twelve organ systems with millions of cells, has a greater capacity to accomplish feats than does the one-cell amoeba. The amoeba moves an inch a day. Humans can not only walk many miles in a day but they can also climb the Cascades, surf the Pacific, and explore the Grand Canyon. The amoeba's sight is crude; it sees faint edges of objects. An amoeba cannot see a spectrum of color. To an amoeba, everything looks flat. Humans see whole objects, the colors of the rainbow, and in three dimensions. A cell standing alone without contact or context has no meaningful work. To paraphrase an old song, cells that need cells are the luckiest cells in the world. Each of our bodies is a community of cells that have come together for a purpose—more life, higher functioning. They haven't come together for less life. Our multicellular bodies are designed for survival *and* growth, both of which are signs of life.

A congregation is a group of people who believe that more can be accomplished by joining with others. They come together with a purpose. To create more life, the people create a community of purpose. After many years of being together, though, people may wonder what happened to the purpose, to the vision, to the creativity, and to the meaningful service that once energized them. This is normal. Again and again, we have to explore why we come together. Congregations need to continue to review who they are and how they will respond. What are we trying to be? What is our calling at this time and in this place? Can we make a difference? Is there a purpose for our presence? If we are unaware of the particular view through which we are looking at the world, then we do not have any true choices about what we are going to see and how we are going to respond.

Mission is the expression of the church's deep, abiding beliefs. Mission provides the major standard against which all activities, services, and decisions are evaluated. Mission is the preserver of congregational integrity. It is about God's love for the world, not about what I like or don't like about my church. A major function of the congregation's stewards is to be the creators and guardians of the mission. They defend the mission against resistant forces that would threaten or destroy it. They oversee the mission's implementation. They keep the mission alive.

This leads us to the next chapter and a view of the time when God will transform the old heaven and earth into the new heaven and earth and will raise up the faithful from the dead to rule over the world he has made and redeemed.

When I first saw a congregation making a significant change by associating that change with mission, I saw far less resistance to the change. In the reverse, I have seen change with no connection to mission easily sabotaged or emotionally resisted. It would make sense, then, to raise the congregation's mission consciousness before embarking on a major shift. I am proposing that congregations put the horse (mission) before the cart (change). Mission carries emotional weight, and it evokes an emotional response. The first step of change—urgency—is built into mission.

CHAPTER 6

JOINING GOD'S NEW CREATION

U nderstanding our hope in the gospel helps us reframe the mission as followers for Jesus. The church's hope for the future is in God, who raised Jesus from the dead. We hope for our own resurrection—"the resurrection of the body" and "life everlasting" (Apostles' Creed). Our hope is never private. We hope for the world, because God, who created the heaven and the earth, will create a new heaven and earth—"his kingdom will have no end" (Nicene Creed). *X*

Popular theology has not always followed traditional thought. Our hope rests on the promise of God to raise us up *bodily*. For instance, our hope is not centered in the indestructible or immortal soul destined for heaven, though popular theology has perpetuated this idea. The Greeks believed the body imprisoned the soul. From this idea, some Christian thinkers extrapolated that death releases an inner divine spark whose battery never runs out and that floats along heavenly streets of gold and other adornments of crystal, halos, and white robes. Salvation, tritely referred to as "going to your rest," is pictured as a continuous holiday in a gated community monitored by St. Pete. Background music is supplied by harps. God performs, in theologian Ted Peters's words, a "soulectomy," separating soul from body for a nonphysical world. So the result is a bodiless person and worldless God. Yes, I have caricatured the afterlife, but caricature or not, some of those notions continue to exist.

God has something far bigger in mind. N. T. Wright explains, "What [Jesus] was promising for that future, and doing in that present, was not saving souls for a disembodied eternity, but rescuing people from the corruption and decay of the way the world presently is so they could enjoy, already in the present, that renewal of creation which is God's ultimate purpose—and so they could thus become colleagues and partners in that larger project."[1] A promise of a new creation and an invitation to a new vocation stretches beyond "me and Jesus" to God's worldwide purposes. The mission of the church must be informed and shaped by how the New Testament presents the future hope.

Seeing Anew

Can we see anew? Plato's cave is an allegory in which the philosopher asked his students to imagine prisoners chained inside a cave, able to face only the wall. For their whole life, all they have seen are the walls and the shadows. Behind them, a fire is burning and puppeteers parade puppets and objects. The fire inside the cave casts the puppets' shadows on the wall. The prisoners think the entire world is black and white, and merely two dimensional.

What would happen, Plato says, if one of the prisoners is unchained, turns around, and heads for the cave's opening? What does the prisoner see? He initially sees Technicolor . . . hues and shades. Color and light, not only shadows. But what are these? Then he goes into the enchanted garden of the world and recognizes that light comes from a source—the sun. "Would he be astonished?" Plato asks. Now, suppose he is taken back inside with his fellow prisoners. He says excitedly, "This isn't all there is. Come, see the bright light." Bringing the story to a close, Plato asks, "What would they think?" He is deranged? Dangerous? If he persisted, the others might do violence against him.

Plato compares the human condition to prisoners chained in a cave. We live in a dimly lit hole with shadowy reflections; we need to open our eyes to larger worlds that have not been known before. An incredible other (sun and light) exists beyond the limiting walls. Turn around. Dare to wake up. Snap the chains. Walk out. Open your eyes.

Allegories carry meaning on many levels. In general, though, interpreters of the myth have cited Plato's belief that truth is universal, not found in the particulars of life. These are mere shadows. Other interpreters mention the mesmerizing effect of what is well known and its deadening effect on wonder. Another interpretation considers the dual possibility that a new discovery can be either liberating or frightening. "Better to attend to the known than to risk the consequences of the unknown," says the fearful heart. "What if something, somehow, will be different?" says the courageous soul.

It seems as if many church people have been living in Plato's cave. They think the church enterprise is about "me." What is at stake is *my* salvation. The me-and-my-salvation individual "does church" by making a fair exchange of time and money for eternal assurances. But the effect of teaching the fate of the individual soul downplays the beginning of God's restoration now. It teaches that the important stuff comes later and that "going to heaven" is the benchmark of Christian life. Yet, the Christian life is so much more than any one person's long-term survival. It is about the world's future; it is about our hope turning our heads and hearts toward the world.

When comedian Stephen Colbert interviewed New Testament scholar N. T. Wright, Colbert said his vision of heaven was a harp, mint julep, and asking Ronald Reagan questions. Farcical as Colbert is, far too many people want to go to heaven for the same reasons many want to go to Hawaii—to enjoy sun, surf, and siesta . . . with a view. But the biblical final destination is a surprise, not merely heaven. It is a new heaven and a new earth. All creation has a future. Our journey in life is not a private affair. We are invited to become agents of God's creative work—seeking the lost, feeding the hungry, and befriending the lonely.

Promise

Anticipating the time when God will fill the earth, transform the old heaven and earth into the new, and revive his children from the dead to inhabit and enjoy the redeemed world he has made, Christians put aside the notions of the church as a place to realize private religious agendas, as a cozy place to escape a crazy world, or as a place where like-minded folks go to receive "message therapy," hearing what they want to hear.

Israel became a community of hope by refusing to allow the exile to be the epitome of their destiny. They confidently trusted that God would in his own time mend the brokenness. They had no FDIC assurances, no natural endowment for rosy expectations, no hope that the law of averages had to play their number eventually—just "My hope is in you" (Ps. 39:7). They did not hope because they had posterity, a deep psychological need to be oriented, or "hope springs eternal" genes. It all came about because of God's *promise* about what he intends to do for and with human history. It is the promise of the good news, of God's will being done on earth as in heaven. Only because God took the *initiative* can we even entertain the possibility of hope. His promise creates the hope, not the need for hope. Our hope is in God's promise to renew all things. The future is different. "The dark door of the future has been thrown open," Pope Benedict XVI declares, "the one who has hope lives differently."[2] We can take our lyres (and guitars, drums, and trumpets) off the trees in this time of dislocation and sing our songs of Zion. Praise rejects despair.

A New Creation

Whenever Israel recited its story of salvation and hope, they pictured a renewal of creation. Their hope for the resurrection of the world had its origin in Israel's faith:

> Behold, I will create
>> new heavens and a new earth.
>
> The former things will not be remembered,
>> nor will they come to mind.
>
> But be glad and rejoice forever
>> in what I will create,
>
> for I will create Jerusalem to be a delight
>> and its people a joy.
>
> —Isa. 65:17–18

Elaborating, the prophet Isaiah envisions the new creation as a startling reversal where the hungry will eat, the sound of weeping will cease, the premature dying of children will end, people who have no place to call home will not be pushed around, and vineyards will produce a surplus of grapes. As a natural sign of this formative handiwork, "The wolf and the lamb will feed together, and the lion will eat straw like the ox" (Isa. 65:25). Accordingly, the people of Israel placed their hope in God's creative action.

The New Testament counterpart to Isaiah is noted in Revelation 21:1–4:

> Then I saw a new heaven and a new earth, for the first heaven and the first earth had passed away, and there was no longer any sea. I saw the Holy City, the new Jerusalem, coming down out of heaven from God, prepared as a bride beautifully dressed for her husband. And I heard a loud voice from the throne saying, "Now the dwelling of God is with men, and he will live with them. They will be his people, and God himself will be with them and be their God. He will wipe

every tear from their eyes. There will be no more death or mourning
or crying or pain, for the old order of things has passed away."

John repeats the themes of Jerusalem's restoration, the covenant's
renewal, grief's cessation, and the former things not counting
anymore. For John, all this centers on "the Lamb of God who
takes away the sin of the world" (John 1:29).

A Kingdom of Peace

The traditional Hebrew term for the future is translated as "the
age to come." Its New Testament companion is the phrase "the
kingdom of God." The relationship between the two is seen in
a comparison of the introductions to kaddish prayer used in the
synagogue and the prayer Jesus taught his disciples:

KADDISH PRAYER

Magnified and sanctified be his great name in the world which he
has created according to his will. May he establish his kingdom in
your lifetime and in your days and in the lifetime of all the house of
Israel speedily and at a near time.[3]

LORD'S PRAYER

Our Father in heaven, hallowed be your name, your kingdom come,
your will be done on earth as it is in heaven. Give us today our daily
bread.

—MATTHEW 6:9–11

Both prayers connect the kingdom of God to the present. The
kingdom of God was the center of the prophetic hope for a
new day of peace, plenty, and mercy, grounded in the Jewish
understanding of God's action in history. Looking forward to a
time when God would transform the whole world, the prophets spoke of shalom, a hope that embraces the well-being of all

things—agricultural bounty, social harmony, and the removal of fear. At one point, the disciples expressed this traditional Jewish hope when they asked Jesus, "Lord, are you at this time going to restore the kingdom to Israel?" (Acts 1:6). The disciples did not realize that the restoration would be far different from what was popularly imagined. Most assumptions clustered around a military victory, a major sign of national superiority, or a well-fortressed city. Speculation could never have predicted that the grand scheme involved a cross and a tomb.

The expectation of a coming kingdom is also evident in the story of two disciples on the road to Emmaus (Luke 24:13–35). They explain the cause for their despondency to a stranger whom they have met. The one they hoped would redeem Israel had been nailed to a cross by the Romans. For them, the ancient hope turned up empty. Only later do they discover that the stranger is Jesus, the very center of the kingdom they hoped for. This kingdom of God will be a kingdom of shalom, of well-being, and of a future. "'For I know the plans I have for you,' declares the LORD, 'plans to prosper [shalom] you and not to harm you, plans to give you hope and a future'" (Jer. 29:11). Theologian Edward Schroeder calls the kingdom of God "God's mercy-management system."

A Sweeping Embrace

With the resurrection of Jesus, everything changes. Both the hope of the resurrection of the dead and the hope for the renewal of the world have been launched. All is redeemed—space, time, matter, people. What is broken in creation will be restored and made whole. God's promise to make all things new embraces everything in creation—the animate and the inanimate, the sea and the mountains, the stars and space. It is cosmic—the whole creation is redeemed. Easter's grand promise is a newly embodied person in a renewed world. German theologian Paul

Althaus wrote that Martin Luther expected the coming restoration of creation, saying, on Luther's thought, "God does not
abandon his creatures and his creation, but transforms, renews,
and glorifies them."[4]

Like Plato's cave dwellers, some people in churches scale down
the cosmic dimension of the resurrection, recognizing only a
private salvation and an interior experience. This narrowed form
of the gospel is a Western phenomenon. Those who first heard
the message, "The kingdom of God is among you" (Luke 17:21
NRSV), understood the "you" as plural. The kingdom refers to
a community. The idea of an interior, private kingdom would
have been totally incoherent to the people of Jesus's time.

Israel's vision of an all-embracing new creation is repeated in
the apostle Paul's claim that the creation itself has been waiting
in eager expectation for the new day. In his words, "We know
that the whole creation has been groaning as in the pains of
childbirth right up to the present time. Not only so, but we
ourselves, who have the firstfruits of the Spirit, groan inwardly
as we wait eagerly for our adoption as sons, the redemption of
our bodies" (Rom. 8:22–23). Surprise! The physical universe is
not sentenced to ultimate destruction but is slated for absolute
renewal. The kingdom of God is this-worldly. A new day is coming when Jews and Gentiles will come together, the outsider will
become the insider, and justice will be the rule, not the exception.

The central point of Easter is that God has set in place his plan
that all things will be put right, set free, and remade. We who
hear the good news are invited to be contributors and designers
of the new creation. Easter is about God's new creation and the
calling of believers to be agents of the kingdom. Christians are
called to embody the hope that the God of promise offers. The
gift of the resurrection provides us with a boldness. We have, as
Martin Luther King Jr. noted, "cosmic allies."

Once out of our own caves, we can identify with what is
other, different, and strange. We see with many eyes, even as

threatening as that may be. Remember Marius von Senden's observation about the difficulties of the blind who receive sight. The newness of hope presents a new world. "But in your hearts set apart Christ as Lord," the apostle Peter announces. "Always be prepared to give an answer to everyone who asks you to give the reason for the hope that you have" (1 Pet. 3:15). The hope we are asked to defend is defined in the Nicene Creed: "We look for the resurrection of the dead and the life of the world to come." Christian hope is no escape or "opiate of the people," as Karl Marx asserts. It allows no room for avoidant behaviors in the messy affairs of life. Christian hope sends us back to life on earth, here and now. Hoping as we do, we are part of a large story where the ending is our beginning, where the future changes the present.

The Christian physicist John Polkinghorne remarked that hope is not a mood but a commitment to action. Its character implies that whatever we hope for we will be prepared to work for, thus bringing it about as we are able. Acknowledging a God who has done a new thing and promises to do so in the future, Polkinghorne urges believers to let their hope become action. As the new creation people, we have a roll-up-your-sleeves hope. We have a destiny to make a difference. Think about N. T. Wright's keen observation:

> Our future beyond death is enormously important, but the nature of the Christian hope is such that it plays back into the present life. We're called, here and now, to be instruments of God's new creation, the world put to rights, which has already been launched in Jesus and of which Jesus' followers are supposed to be not simply beneficiaries but also agents.[5]

In Wright's terms, no one can make a defense for the hope that is in them apart from putting their hope into action. The living hope of Christians is the basis of Christian mission. It is hope for the poor, the sick, the despairing, the stranger, the homeless, the hungry, the sinner, the neglected, the embittered, and those shackled in their own paranoia. Martin Luther called faith "a busy, active thing." And if hope is faith on tiptoes, hope is never quiet but quite restless, itching to go, and ready to serve. As long as there is poverty, disease, unemployment, despair, and the like, the voice of God asks the primal question, "Where are you?" God would have our hope meet the world's needs.

The esteemed missionary and theologian Lesslie Newbigin says no one can say "Thy will be done on earth as it is in heaven" with sincere faith if they have no interest in making that will visible in action. By God's action, we are set free from sin and death to play our true part in love and service.

Many Voices

The earth is hope's theater where we play out God's future in the present. Theologians from many different viewpoints come together and join in concert about the meaning of Easter:

JURGEN MOLTMANN: "Far from leading human beings away from earth and heaven, the Christian hope leads them to the Kingdom of God, which comes on earth."[6]

JOEL B. GREEN: "We are not rescued from the cosmos in resurrection, but transformed with it in new creation."[7]

TED PETERS: "As I have been suggesting, human destiny is inseparable from cosmic destiny. . . . To understand the resurrected Body, we need to place it within the broader horizon of God's new creation. As the creation is transformed, so are we."[8]

RICHARD JOHN NEUHAUS: "There is no vindication of the self in isolation from the world of which we are part. Again, the words of

> John—'*God so loved the world*—that he gave his only Son . . .' It is in
> the redemption of the world, not in disengagement from the world,
> that we seek our own redemption" (emphasis added).[9]

A pair of conservative theologians contest the me-and-Jesus mentality that persists within some parts of their circles. Carl F. H. Henry states, "There is no room . . . for a gospel that is indifferent to the needs of the total man, nor of the global man." In reference to the Great Commission, John Stott insists that "The actual commission itself must be understood to include social as well as evangelical responsibility, unless we are to be guilty of distorting the words of Jesus."[10]

Speaking from a viewpoint of the developing nations, South African theologian H. Russel Botman proposes, "God does not want and did not plan on having a future separate from or without creation."[11] Instead, Botman asserts that the act of the resurrection and the kingdom of God mean that God has selected this world for fulfilling his gracious promises.

The Old-Time Religion

Darrell Guder, a professor at Princeton Seminary, notes that opposition to the making of a mission culture will come from within the community of faith. He says it is possible not to hear the gospel in terms of the kingdom of God. Many are still on the self-survival bandwagon; they see the church being about "my aches and pains and sorrows" and "going to heaven" in the future. Congregations, he believes, are not preparing people to be a blessing, only to receive the benefits.[12]

As a result, mission becomes a slogan or a program or a word devoted to the saving of souls. But this old-time religion is an emotional barrier to mission. The biblical message is misunderstood to be primarily about *my* needs. The message is taken off the therapeutic shelf, emphasizing utilitarian ends and

Figure **6.1.** The Old-Time Church and the New Creation

HOPEFULNESS	THE OLD-TIME CHURCH	THE NEW CREATION
Purpose	To save souls	To be raised from the dead with a new body and to participate in God's renewal of heaven and earth
Body-Soul Connection	The soul is separate (be wary of the bodily and material world)	The creature is a whole being (body, mind, and spirit)
Self and Others	Isolated individual	Self has meaning only in relationship to all things (social, relational, political)
Relationship to the World	In, but not of, the world	In, and for, the world.
Relationship to Time	Then/Later	Both now and not yet
Activity of Faith	Faith is private, personal, and internal	Faith is trust in God's mercy and becomes active in love
Eschatology	Only the future counts	The future promises change the present
What Counts	Going to heaven	Joining in God's new creation

bestowing satisfaction, which are not directly promised by God. For example, Pastor Joel Osteen's *Your Best Life Now* is about being only a beneficiary, hardly a blessing. Even Rick Warren's bestseller—*The Purpose Driven Church*—is introduced with the promise, "Having this perspective will reduce your stress, simplify your decisions, increase your satisfaction."[13] If only Abraham, Moses, or Jacob had it so good, no less the martyrs of the early church.

To join God's new creation means that we must leave the cave. Inside, the vision is narrow; it's all about *me*. We need to look for the door marked "A New Heaven and a New Earth." It has been set open, for the new creation is God's yes to the world. The old-time religion—gospel as commodity, gospel as a private affair, gospel not as good news but as good therapy—is a half gospel. To be part of the new creation is not to be sure that the reservation on the eternity list for our soul alone has not expired or been lost. The kingdom of God is not the same as the triumph of the therapeutic. To be part of the new creation is to be part of the Big Surprise—a whole new earth. No one who buys into the me-and-Jesus concept will ever ask, "Have you taken Jesus as your hope for the resurrection and the transformation of the world?" Old-time religion narrows the question down to a "personal" Savior.

N. T. Wright outlines in a positive way the true vocation of those who trust God's promises:

> Every act of love, gratitude, and kindness; every work of art or music inspired by the love God and delight in the beauty of his creation, . . . every act of care and nurture, of comfort and support, for one's fellow human beings and for that matter one's fellow nonhuman creatures; and of course, every prayer, all Spirit-led teaching, every deed that spreads the gospel, builds up the church, embraces and embodies holiness rather than corruption, and makes the name of Jesus honored in the world—all of this will find its way, through the resurrecting power of God, into the new creation that God will one day make. That is the logic of the mission of God.[14]

God is a God of promise not of bargains. Where our hope centers on God's promise, we hope for the whole fragile but precious world created by the promiser.

PART III

THE RESPONSE

WITH JESUS, GOD'S rescue operation has been put into effect once and for all. A great door has swung open in the cosmos, which can never again be shut. It's the door to the prison where we've been kept chained up. We are offered freedom: freedom to experience God's resurrection for ourselves, to go through the open door and explore the new world to which we now have access. In particular, we are all invited—summoned continually—to discover, through following Jesus, that this new world is indeed a place of justice, spirituality, relationship, and beauty, and that we are not only to enjoy it as such, but to work at bringing it to birth on earth as in heaven

—N. T. WRIGHT
Simply Christian

Chapter 7

The People of the Way

*I*n her book *Pilgrim at Tinker Creek*, poet and essayist Annie Dillard quotes a woman who said, "Seem like we're just set down here, and don't nobody know why." Asking why we exist has been an inexhaustible question for both philosophers and the common citizen. What is it all about? Dillard adds her own twist to the woman's comment: "Some unwonted, taught pride diverts us from our original intent," she writes, "which is to explore the neighborhood, view the landscape, to discover at least where it is that we have been so startlingly set down, even if we can't learn why."[1] She shifts the question from, "Why in the world do we exist?" to "Where in the world are we going?"

If indeed we North American Christians are living in a time of exile or dislocation or a time when things are up in the air, it is an opportune time to ask, Where are we? Where are we going? If we are going to know where we are, we have to explore the neighborhood.

Smart Moves

One could say we are "set down here" to explore. Why else would each of us have a brain? The brain, most people would say, is for thinking. Do something foolish and someone might curtly remark, "Don't you have any brains?" But *think* again. The primary purpose of the brain is to choose and regulate our movement; it is also designed to detect the movements of other living things and objects. Under the brain's direction, three sets of moveable body parts function—legs, feet, and toes; arms, hands, and fingers; face, neck, and tongue. "It is not our feet that move us along," the ancient Chinese proverb attests, "it is our minds."

In contrast, a plant is a living organism that lacks a brain. Plants are not going anywhere of their own choice. Award-winning writer Jay Griffiths, from Wales, writes, "Trees can't run. Ah, but they can worry." German foresters have discovered that some trees develop "anxiety shoots." To compensate for the damage wrought by air pollution, new shoots jet out of the tree trunk. Worry they may, but they have no idea where they are. And what would be the point? They have nowhere to go.[2]

The word *animus* means "mind" and is the root word from which are hewn the words *animal* and *animation*. Living animals walk, chew, and jump. Propelling air molecules out of their mouths, human beings move thoughts from their brains into the ears and brains of others. Breathing, speaking, and singing are as much forms of movement as lifting or bending. When movement stops, life ends. We even refer colloquially to a dead person as a "stiff." When living beings are surprised, becoming motionless, we say they were "caught dead in their tracks." They stopped moving. Our everyday expressions contain other words indicating a cessation in movement, from *deadline* to *deadbeat*, *dead ball* to *deadlock*. Movement is associated with life. In our neurological makeup, we are designed to crawl, climb, and leap.

Watching individuals who are capable of moving fast or adroitly, and others who can move objects with great velocity or for a long distance, thrills us. We enjoy seeing people's movements to avoid obstacles, reach a finish line, or execute graceful motions. And because of the worldwide fascination with these movements, we turn them into performances and games called the Olympics.

More than we realize, movement is connected to learning. Neurophysiologist Carla Hannaford asserts, "Movement, a natural process, is now understood to be essential to learning, creative thought, and higher level forms of reasoning."[3] With movement, the neural wiring in one's body is activated, and the whole body becomes part of learning. John Melinda, author of *Brain Rules*, calls physical activity "cognitive candy." As Ella Fitzgerald used to sing, "It don't mean a thing, if it ain't got that swing."

The Movement

Movement is central to an understanding of *mission*, meaning "send out." God made the first move in his promises, and invites us to respond movingly. Movement is a significant part of both biblical content and spiritual living. Adam and Eve are extradited from Eden. Under the burden of Pharaoh, the people of Israel escape by way of the sea and wander in the wilderness for four decades, giving the second book of the Bible the title "Exodus" (departure). The Lord instructs Abraham to go to the land that he will show him. The builders of the Tower of Babel are scattered to the winds. Reluctantly, Jonah proceeds to Nineveh. The exile to Babylon was an unwanted movement. In the New Testament, Mary and Joseph go to Bethlehem and flee to Egypt. Jesus spends three years on the road. When one of his disciples has a deep spiritual experience on a mountaintop and wants to build a settlement of booths, Jesus refuses the offer and returns to the valley where he heals a young boy.

Jesus inspired the start of a movement, subsequently named "The Way." Christianity did not begin as an organization. In the beginning, a scattering of people and small groups—the twelve, his family (Mary, James, Jude), his friends Mary and Martha, certainly some of society's poor people, and even a Pharisee— were drawn to Jesus. In the early first century, the number of adherents might have been two to five thousand people who met in people's homes and shops.

The movement had no doctrines, no consensus on how to live, no prescribed liturgy to follow, no physical location for cohesion (like Rome), just the incredible impact Jesus had on their lives and the conviction that his spirit moved among them. The earliest creed consisted of the confession "Jesus is Lord." When the time came to support the movement, four small books called Gospels appeared. Their purpose was to show how Jesus was relevant to people who lived outside of Palestine a generation after Jesus's death.

On the Move

For a long time, I did not comprehend the phrase in the Apostles' Creed—"the quick and the dead." Now, of course, it makes sense: the quick are the living, which is the word used in newer translations. Only the living can move. Sydney Carter, who wrote the hymn "The Lord of the Dance," composed songs that depict life as a journey. Once, he remarked:

> Everything is traveling: there is no way out of it. But there are different ways of doing it. You can travel inertly like a stone which is hurled in the air. You can travel reluctantly like a dog which drags against the lead. You can embrace the necessity of traveling: you can leap and dance along.
>
> The kingdom of heaven (if you like) or God: it lies ahead of us, yet it travels in us too. . . . We are pulled in two directions, and we have a choice. We are privileged or condemned to be free. We can drag or dance along.[4]

The kingdom of God is shorthand for God setting into motion a plan to mend life—"It lies ahead of us," writes Carter. But it also "travels in us" as we explore the neighborhood. "The resurrection narratives depict a God who is constantly on the move, energetic, revealing here, now." Methodist Bishop William Willimon affirms: "Easter stories depict a God who refuses to stop talking and cease walking."[5] As Carter proposes, we can live our Christian lives in one of three ways: inertly, reluctantly, or freely. Our lives can be *inert*, uninspired, a passive going-through-the-motions with no thought or choice of our own that thrusts us forward. Or we can move *reluctantly*; that is, only if we are nudged or badgered. Our heart either is not in it or less than half of it is. The third movement is *freedom*, being a willing and engaged participant. We dance with the stars.

In addition to the three movements Carter lists, I propose a fourth movement related to bacteria that I referred to earlier—*tumbling*. The church is now in a place where the future is unclear. The church is in limbo. Medieval theologians characterized heaven as assurance, hell as despair, and limbo as uncertainty. Anxiety intensifies when certainty is absent. Many anxious church people see the church heading downhill, slipping off to the sidelines, and tumbling. We need to remember that tumbling, though it is not directed, is the very condition necessary to adjust course. When the flagella of bacteria lose the scent of food, they change direction (move clockwise) in order to go into a tailspin in search of a strong scent (visiting the neighborhood).

Transition

William Bridges, a consultant on transition management, says change is an event. Our *experience* of the change is transition. He cites three movements—endings, the neutral zone, and beginnings—in the transition experience:

> All we know is that periodically, some situation or event deflects us from the path that we thought we were on, and, in so doing, ends the life-chapter we were in. In order to continue our journey, we are forced to let go of the way we got that far. Having let go, we find

ourselves in the wilderness for a time, and until we have lived out that time can we come back around to a new beginning.[6]

Many cultural historians believe we in the West are living between two eras, witnessing the end of the life chapter that has held for centuries. The conventional and familiar props of established society are rapidly disappearing. With the ending of a way of life, people are pursuing safety and stability that are not yet available. We are entering the "wilderness for a time."

Bridges notes that both people and organizations try to steer clear of the neutral zone. By doing so, we turn what could be a developmental transition into a reactive one. In a developmental transition, all shifts and novelties become opportunities for new thinking and new movements. In a reactive transition, we keep one foot in the old era. We refuse to let go. Bridges mentions that we don't realize that consciousness of an ending is the beginning of renewal: there once was a world; it's gone. By acknowledging an ending, we enter the slippery slope of the neutral zone. Here, we go through the tumble, which can make us feel out of control and a bit crazy. We are tempted to turn what could be a learning experience (developmental transition) into a stubborn defense of what one has always believed (reactive transition). Nothing is more important to us than abbreviating the time we spend in the wilderness. Transitions, however, are immune to watches and calendars.

Bridges alludes to a second temptation, which he calls the "additive fallacy." We think that if we add and add, for example, data, goods, services, and people, we will finish up with something more enduring or stronger. Edwin Friedman spoke about an odd pairing—maturity versus data. He contended that people usually believe *more*, particularly more data, will solve problems. But facts—no matter how many one introduces—do not motivate people to change. Friedman suggests we spend less effort in spawning data and more in helping individuals mature.

FIGURE 7.1. TRANSITION—THE EXPERIENCE OF CHANGE

ENDING	NEUTRAL ZONE	BEGINNING
Feels like failure	As if in a tunnel	New directions
Reminder of death	"Betwixt and between"	See a path
Fear of the unknown	Twilight zone	Reorientation
Loss of coherency	Wilderness	Reframe
Broken connections	Experience of nowhere	Ripening, maturing
Doesn't know the way	Edge of chaos	Surprising events
Reactivity	Liminal	Opportunity
"Additive fallacy"	"A deep, drizzly	Hope
Disorientation	November in my soul"	Dancing again
Old-identity shaken	Potential for learning	
	As if nothing is happening	

Being increasingly responsible and responsive to what is there is far more significant than a pile of information.[7]

In the transition-turmoil of today's church, many have regarded church growth as the fix for the current shrinkage in membership and worship attendance. To fortify the claim, they have cited Matthew 28:18–20, what is called the Great Commission. Earlier in this book, I inferred that Matthew 28 may be broader in meaning than the sheer addition of attendees. We have to, at times, tumble; it has its merits. Theologian Joseph Sittler called the neutral zone a "germinating darkness." Jesus himself suggested that thinking about a new future is best understood using organic metaphors like mustard seeds and vines, images that portray a ripening, a gradual maturation, and a deepening. More of anything is not the answer to transitional times—not more data, not more numbers. Worse, the additive fallacy can prevent the developing process, the new beginnings. The neutral zone, chaotic as it may be, is the source of revitalization. In Hebrew, the word for crisis is *mashber*, meaning "birth stool."

Like in nature, growth in the church begins with pressure, some sort of pushing out or some kind of tension.

What Friedman suggests, as opposed to more data, is elevating the level of people's maturity, their capacity to respond rather than react, to reflect instead of defend, and to choose wisely rather than jump on a bandwagon. What Friedman suggests is explicit in Matthew 28:18–20: the instruction to "make disciples." Disciples are learners—explorers, actors, and creators. Or to put it in a simple way: What would we rather have, one disciple and fifty members or five disciples and ten members?

Process

The *process* of ripening may be as or more important than the *outcome* or production, such as data or numbers. Bridges is quite emphatic:

> If there is one thing that the way of transition and the path of the life-journey teach, it is that . . . when we neglect the process and try instead to copy the outcome, we fail completely to get what we were after. Copying always creates something that is dead, because it simplifies the original and does not arise from the real creativity that is always present when real people are in an actual neutral zone.[8]

Anxious people look outside of themselves for relief. They may hanker for a technique that will bring about results they want to achieve; they want to replicate what has been discovered by someone else: "Give me a copy of the wonderful plans." Seeing what those plans have done for others, they want the same result—but without going through the process that got the others to that point. The shortcut of imitation certainly bypasses a lot of pain. How churches hunger for precisely this situation! No tumbling.

Meaningful, lasting outcomes are the result of the journey and the learning that takes place. Maybe a word of caution should be stamped on all programs: "Not transferable." Transition time, especially the neutral zone experience, is life's curriculum. Being on the path opens new insight; being on the path, not the steps one takes, is the very condition necessary for learning. Tumbling is disruptive but equally instructive.

The Bible is replete with stories of transition, exile, and tumbling. Jacob, who was always a wimpy character, is on his way to meet the brother he tricked and fooled. He struggles with an angel on the wet banks of the Jabbok River, and out of the struggle finds strength to meet his brother. Jesus spends forty days in the wilderness—alone, hungry, numb—and the devil tempts him three times. The process of thinking, testing, and exploring contains the lessons. Churches need to remember that no handbook is available on freelancing mission. Only by going out, being there, and seeing from a fresh angle will the process lead to learning. Discovering how to *respond* to shifts and changes is the learning. Self-confidence is a byproduct. But growth is in the struggle, the push, and the journey. Churches in decline need to look beyond the BIG RESULT and become the people of the way—tumble and all.

Moving Ahead

Friedman tells the story of the Holy One approaching his creatures before all forms of life are about to multiply in the creation story from Genesis: "I see that what some of you treasure most is survival, while what others yearn for most is adventure. So I will give you each a choice. If what you want most is stability, then I will give you the power to regenerate any part you lose, but you must stay rooted where you grow. If, on the other hand, you prefer mobility, you also may have your wish, but you will be more at risk. For then I will not give you the ability to regain your previous form."[9] Those that chose stability we call trees, and those that chose opportunity became animals.

Movement favors opportunity, new beginnings, and exploration. But it comes, as Friedman notes, with more risk. Movement, if emotionally resisted, will not be easy street. New beginnings can certainly become lonesome trails as people opt out of the venture. In fact, the word *travel* comes from the French *travailler*, meaning to labor or work with difficulty. In modern English, the word *travail* is often a reference to labor pains in childbirth. Nonetheless, movement is for mobility, opportunity, moving ahead, blazing a new path. Perhaps we should place a sign somewhere in the church building or on the grounds that says, "For Adventurers Only."

After years of working with organizations, Friedman saw a common denominator in well-functioning groups or organizations. It was the spirit of adventure, where people have courage, where we are open to new possibilities, where we are willing to try things we never thought of trying before, and where, for a period of time, we are willing to tumble.

The door is set open. "O God, our help in ages past" will be "our hope for years to come."[10] We know something about the future—with all its uncertainties—and that is, we can trust the future because God has kept his promises in the past.

Are we a people of the way or in the way? Are you ready to explore the neighborhood?

Chapter 8

WHERE TO TOUCH
THE ELEPHANT

*T*he well-known story of the elephant and the blind men has several versions. One version goes like this: a group of blind men touch an elephant to learn what it is like. Each one, though, touches a different part of the animal, and, based on that part, infer a larger truth about what the entire elephant must be like. In one account, the elephant is like a wicker basket to the one who touched the ear, a pot to the blind man who touched the head, and a brush to the one who touched the tip of the tail. When they compare their experiences, they discover their disagreement. Each one has his own view of reality, depending upon where he touched the elephant. Someone once said that truth is like an elephant surrounded by blind men.

Picking up on this story, Edwin Friedman states, "I touch the elephant wherever the elephant appears."[1] His remark is based on the idea that the enormity of the elephant precludes anyone comprehending the whole. One can only observe what is there in front of him or her. In life, Friedman is suggesting, prodigious complexity can be understood only from the perspective of what is at hand. The elephant is too monstrous to handle in its entirety.

Let's probe the elephant-touch dilemma as it affects the life of today's church: If we think of the elephant as representing the congregation's mission, do all touches have the same value? Is there a place we all must touch? Finally, can we touch the mission in different places, disagree, and still work together?

Applying the elephant rule to life, one cannot deal with everything; therefore, one must work with what is at hand or known. The same rule applies to the church. Touch whatever aspect of mission is within reach. No congregation has to cover every part of the elephant. Even a congregation that has created and sustained a deep sense of mission has to work within a limited scope. Leaders and members need to humbly recognize they are not God's only agent of renewal in the neighborhood. Every congregation in town is on the contributors' list. Alongside churches are other donors. Resources are not evenly distributed among congregations; some congregations have more "outputs" than others. If a congregation thinks its outputs are secondary or paltry compared to others, it needs to remember the widow's mite. Her contribution affirms that proportion can be as important as total amount. Besides, the immense, widespread human needs that summon our attention and gifts can overwhelm us. A small church may feel that their personal and financial offerings are inconsequential. Some people may conclude that the part of mission they have touched is the responsibility of another institution. A congregation may limit itself to its own kind. Worse yet, people may indicate that mission is none of their concern: There is no elephant in the room.

Yet all congregations need to touch *tikkun olam*, a Jewish concept that means "to mend the world." It epitomizes God's work. Theologian and poet Howard Thurman set the mending motif into a memorable frame, with the birth of Jesus as background:

The Work of Christmas
When the song of the angels is stilled,
    When the star in the sky is gone,
When the kings and princes are home,
    When the shepherds are back with their flock,
The work of Christmas begins,
    To find the lost,

To heal the broken,
　To feed the hungry,
To release the prisoner,
　To rebuild the nations,
To bring peace among brothers,
　To make music in the heart.[2]

All the movements of angels, kings, and shepherds foreshadow the "work of Christmas," the mending of the world.

N. T. Wright elaborates: "What you do in the present—by painting, preaching, singing, sewing, praying, teaching, building hospitals, digging wells, campaigning for justice, writing poems, caring for the needy, loving your neighbor as yourself—*will last into God's future*."[3] Whatever we do to mend the world has lasting value. Everyone contributes. God blesses each and every gift.

One by One

No gifts are undervalued in the new creation. We in the church have tasks to do. We are encouraged to "give [ourselves] fully to the work of the Lord" (1 Cor. 15:58), for whatever we do in the name of the Lord will benefit others. It counts. Go to it. "Strengthen the weak hands and make firm the feeble knees" (Isa. 35:3 NRSV). It counts. No gift, no mending, is too little.

Anthropologist Loren Eiseley tells a story about an elderly man who observed a young man on the beach at dawn. Littered by the retreating tide, the beach contained thousands of starfish. One by one, the young man stooped down and threw them back into the sea. Going to the young man, the senior gentleman asked why he was pitching the starfish back to their natural home. "If left exposed," the young man said, "the sun would kill them." "But the beach extends for miles with thousands of starfish," the older man protested. "Do you think you'll make a difference?" Looking at the starfish in his hand, the young man exclaimed, "To this one, it makes a difference."[4] Everything counts. Tikkun olam involves one starfish at a time, one hungry person at a time, one opportunity to bring cheer to the despondent at a time. Touch the mission where it appears. And one and one and one and one can amount to a great deal.

We are invited to be part of tikkun olam—repairing that which is broken—one by one, for tikkun olam is an expression of the hope that is in us. Here and now, we have opportunity to make a contribution to what needs to be done. We set up signposts of the coming new creation with each act of love, whether it is welcoming the stranger, forgiving one another, or telling the story of God's redemption. A time is coming, not yet apparent, when the abuse of the vulnerable, the neglect of children, and the building of refugee camps will be replaced by God's shalom. Fully convinced that because God is God, we act in his name for the other's sake, knowing it will "last into God's future."

Each person participates in the mending assignment in his or her own way. Also, each congregation subscribes to a specific way of mending. Thus, some people seek to change policies that disregard people's dignity. Yet others become quiet helpers and caring friends. A portion of the congregation enjoys teaching the gospel. A smaller number serve with their prophetic voices. Tikkun olam embraces small gifts and large ones. Your response of mercy, generous offerings, or shared witness makes a difference. In no way is God's future dependent on our offerings, but the new creation is open to all gifts of our hands and hearts. We are part of God's creative scheme when we care for something larger than ourselves. What could be more creative than to see the image of Christ in the face of the stranger or hear Christ's voice in the cry of the starving child?

The Poor

From a biblical perspective, the kingdom of God gives special attention to the poor. The term *poor* as used in the Scriptures does not necessarily indicate economic deprivation. It is a term for an aggregate of human conditions: blind, lame, lepers, hungry, beggars, sick, sinners (meaning those whose work did not meet the standards of the law, such as tax collectors and prostitutes), and unskilled day laborers. Included in the poor are widows and orphans, who had no social standing or rights. These people had to struggle with being without honor, being social outcasts, being grossly dependent, being easily victimized, and being wracked by shame. One Pharisee refers to them as "this mob that knows nothing of the law—there is a curse on them" (John 7:49). Their importance cannot be lost, because the Old Testament refers to them roughly 250 times. The poor, vulnerable to threat, violence, and neglect, need an advocate. No less than the creator of the universe is in the forefront of their cause:

> He who is kind to the poor lends to the LORD (Prov. 19:17).
> He who oppresses the poor shows contempt for their Maker, but whoever is kind to the needy honors God (Prov. 14:31).
> He defends the cause of the fatherless and the widow, and loves the alien, giving him food and clothing. And you are to love those who are aliens, for you yourselves were aliens in Egypt (Deut. 10:18–19).

In the New Testament, Jesus's ministry continues the Old Testament theme. He lived among the downtrodden and disenfranchised. He fed the hungry, healed the sick, relieved the demon-possessed, and preached good news to the poor. When John the Baptist's emissaries ask Jesus if he is the Messiah, Jesus says to them: "Go back and report to John what you have seen and heard: The blind receive sight, the lame walk, those who have leprosy are cured, the deaf hear, the dead are raised" (Luke 7:22). Jesus became an outcast by association, putting him in conflict with the benefactors of the system, both religious and political. But the *crowds* eagerly received and listened to him. "A large crowd gathered around him" (Mark 5:21). "The large crowd listened to him with delight" (Mark 12:37). Jesus was their voice; he was their hope. But the keepers and successors of the present order were terrified, thinking only how to sabotage him. Enter—the emotional process:

> But they were furious and began to discuss with one another what they might do to Jesus (Luke 6:11).
> Then the Pharisees went out and began to plot with the Herodians how they might kill Jesus (Mark 3:6).
> And they plotted to arrest Jesus in some sly way and kill him (Matt. 26:4).

But the eager crowd heard that there would be a reversal of fortunes:

> Blessed are you who are poor for yours is the kingdom of God (Luke 6:20).
> Do not be afraid, little flock, for your Father has been pleased to give you the kingdom (Luke 12:32).

In the new creation, the future will be where *service* supplants *domination*, *equal sharing* displaces *one-sided advantages*, and *love* trumps *manipulation*.

South African bishop Desmond Tutu reminds us that every one of us is God's stand-in. "Everyone, everyone, without exception, everyone, even the most unlikely, even the most undeserving" are "God-carriers" or "God's stand-ins" too.[5] Jesus taught his followers about the coming great judgment: "'Lord, when did we see you hungry and feed you, or thirsty and give you something to drink? When did we see you a stranger and invite you in, or needing clothes and clothe you? When did we see you sick or in prison and go to visit you?' The King will reply, 'I tell you the truth, whatever you did for one of the least of these brothers of mine, you did for me'" (Matt. 25:37–40). Among the promises of God are his presence—whenever two or three are gathered together in his name, until the end of the ages, and among the poor.

God is active in behalf of the well-being of the world, especially those whose well-being is most tenuous. The God–neighbor relationship is elemental to mission. Long ago, Augustine remarked that anyone thinking they had understood the divine Scriptures but unable to see the "two-fold life of God and neighbor," had not really understood them. No wonder Rowan Williams, archbishop of Canterbury, exclaims that the motto of the church is "Not without the others."

Back to the Future

Imagine an assembly of ancient Jews. With a scroll in his hands, the reader puts forth Psalm 146:7–10 (NRSV):

> The LORD sets the prisoners free;
>> the LORD opens the eyes of the blind.
> The LORD lifts up those who are bowed down.
>> The LORD loves the righteous;
> The LORD watches over the strangers;
>> he upholds the orphan and the widow,
>> but the way of the wicked he brings to ruin.
> The LORD will reign forever.

What have the assembled listeners heard? They hear that God mends the world so that the broken creation becomes the new creation God has always intended. And they hear that God's action is on behalf of the whole. God's action is *social*.

Suppose a person in that assembly told someone else that he has had a religious experience of high emotion, that he had attained the secret to religious knowledge, or that, because of his earnest faith, he had been given an abundance of wealth. The person he told might say she is pleased he had those experiences. But, after hearing this psalm, she might also rightfully ask him, "What about your neighbor? What about peace? And justice? The hungry? Are these not also God's work? Have you been touching only one part of the elephant?"

Differences and Differing

We have explored where the church needs to touch mission. Next, we will consider what happens when we touch different parts and disagree about the nature of mission. Which part of the elephant best represents the elephant? In our society, we are increasingly clustering into like-minded groups. The big tent where people could openly express diverse views is giving way to small groups of like-mindedness. People are herded into the cramped space of special interests or value issues or partisan positions. Then, too often, we handle our disagreements aggressively, even viciously.

Friedman noted that differences, by themselves, do not create differing. Our clashes are the result of rising anxiety. Polarization is emotionally maintained. The conflict has little to do with where I am touching the elephant. It is not about whether the elephant is a basket, bowl, or brush. It is about the grip of my emotionality on my functioning. To their misfortune, churches are imitating the wider society and resorting to the ideologue's frame of reference—either–or, this or that, and black or white— which is in reality an emotional reaction. Let me illustrate this in the following case study.

Valley Church appeared to be one of the least likely of congregations to be subject to conflict. Signs of health, growth, satisfaction—or whatever measure one uses to assess a congregation—were all there. A new pastor, whom I will call Rex, had received a warm welcome. Valley Church had grown from two hundred to five thousand members during the twenty-five-year term of Rex's predecessor. By the end of Rex's first year, the congregation had grown nearly 10 percent, and a major new facility was about to be constructed. Under the calm veneer, however, discontent was brewing. The governing board was stunned when a group of unhappy members formed. As surprising as the resistance itself was, who the resisters were compounded the bewilderment.

Two laypeople who had held principal positions of leadership during the previous years had been replaced in the new leadership structure. Well-connected, the pair began to solicit support to have their roles restored. They assembled some people who were not pleased with Rex for other reasons, and they began to meet privately. They called themselves the Progressives, an ironic name, given that the two wanted to go back in time. A book of complaints was compiled. Eventually, they sent it to the board for action.

The congregation's leaders did not know the true number of people who attended the Progressives' meetings, but the best guess was fifty people. The group was not just "anybodies," but "stalwarts" of the congregation. Though only about 1 percent of the whole, they had influence way beyond their numbers. Consequently, the board invited them to speak about their unhappiness, primarily with Rex. After a few weeks, the board chose not to address the book of complaints. But the group's lamenting now took on a strong emotional tone, becoming shrill. Soon, the board asked for my assistance. My associate and I interviewed about fifty people, including the Progressives, the staff, and the board members.

I think that I have done this work long enough to distinguish legitimate complaints from what I call "off-the-shelf complaints." The latter are predictable, commonplace, and overdrawn. To me, the book of complaints was full of off-the-shelf issues. I have said previously that I believe there is a book out there called *ZAP*, an acronym for "Zingers Against Pastors." Its advice goes something like this: If you want to zing your pastor, be sure to begin with, "The pastor doesn't care," and give only *one* example. To top things off, let others know that "I am not being spiritually fed," as if that is the pastor's full responsibility. The unhappy group at Valley Church must have read *ZAP*.

I began to understand what was behind all the clamor. Primarily, the eruption began with the reorganization that dismissed two lay leaders from their positions. It was clearly not done maliciously. But they were not able to work through the loss of their positions, the ending part of the transition process. Instead, they protested by giving grievances and assembling allies. Nothing but restitution to their former positions would satisfy them. I gave my report to a gathering of Progressives, board members, and most of the staff. I presented a dozen observations, raised three questions, and suggested several processes for handling the situation. Not satisfied, a few Progressives accused me of failing to see through the dangers of Rex's new vision, of reinterpreting their comments, and of not excoriating Rex for marginalizing *some* leaders—two, in fact. Some left the meeting crying, others exasperated, and many embarrassed by the behaviors of members of their own group. Some had hoped to reduce their tension by the this-or-that mode of resolution: simply, *this* is wrong; *that* is right.

The board convened afterwards, and their anxiety about the unhappiness had increased. Having encountered the continued resistance of the Progressives first, I now encountered the new resistance of board members. A few complained that no specific advice was given in the report on how to satisfy the Progressives. A couple were upset that the Progressives had left with emotional outbursts and faulted my report for inciting their feelings. Making little progress that evening, I suggested a time-out and said I would return in a couple of weeks to finish the process so that they could make good decisions for themselves.

The next day, Rex forwarded to me a series of e-mails addressed to him and board members. The first e-mail came from a board member who also happened to be the spouse of one of the displaced leaders. He disagreed with my report, but never gave any indication why, and asked that the board dismiss me, adding a few pejorative labels for me. The person who sent the second e-mail said the group had agreed unanimously to hire me, and therefore this person recommended my return. The chair of the board, who had contemplated resigning, sent the third e-mail, in which he said that he had reread my report and that it held up a mirror to them that they didn't like (they were delaying a response to the Progressives for fear of negative reactions), and that this was why people wanted to dispose of me. Quite clearly he said that he was inviting me back. The writer of the first e-mail, in the meantime, resigned. I did return. With the emotional resistance turned down, the leaders, like cream, rose to the top. For one thing, anxiety had less of a grip on them. Anxiety makes people dumber. We suffer imagination gridlock. The board started offering sensible approaches because, instead of focusing on the reactivity of others, they began to self-reflect on what had happened. The pivotal moment came when a physician on the board offered her opinion about the experience. In essence, she said:

> We are responsible for deciding whether or not the complaints of the Progressives are legitimate. From the beginning, we didn't think so. To verify our hunches, we hired a consultant. He laid it out clearly. At first, we were emotionally stuck, because the unhappy people are still unhappy. Many of them we know, love, and respect. My best friend is one of them. Our responsibility is not to please them or take care of their unhappiness. We have been fair, patient, and respectful. But the mission of this church supercedes anyone's or any group's loss or emotionality.

The board moved from being anxious about the anxiety of others to focusing on its responsibility. The board members were able to sustain their unity in the midst of an emotionally charged disagreement without shunning, humiliating, or demonizing each other or the complainants. (The only exception was the board member whose spouse lost a key position.) Situations like this give the church a magnificent opportunity to disagree profoundly over matters without turning away from one another or turning against one another.

More Than

Church members can easily forget behavior is as much an expression of what one believes as it is content. In the Sermon on the Mount, Jesus asks bluntly, "If you love those who love you, what reward do you have? Do not even the tax collectors do the same? And if you greet only your brothers and sisters, what more are you doing than others? Do not even Gentiles do the same?" (Matt. 5:46–47 NRSV).

"What more are you doing than others?" This is the context in which the church must consider Luke 14:13–14—"But when you give a banquet, invite the poor, the crippled, the lame, the blind, and you will be blessed." They cannot repay you. Your gift is unconditional. And it is the context for understanding Ephesians 2:2—"Be completely humble and gentle; be patient, bearing with one another in love."

We fail to be the agents of God's mission because we do not know how to answer the blunt question: What more are you doing than others? What we forget is that a congregation's public face is part of the mission. What do people see when we are at odds? When we are loaded with anxiety? Outside the community of faith, people don't have a whole lot of interest in our mission statements, only our mission practices. We will from time to time touch the elephant in different places. Indeed, we can fight it out as we would in any other place. Perhaps a more mature response would be, "I don't agree, but the mission takes precedence over my self-interests."

CHAPTER 9

A DIFFERENT FUTURE

A Zen saying instructs, "After enlightenment, the laundry." After the illumination, the discovery, and the learning moments, it is time to turn to *RO*—the response of the organism. The laundry symbolizes reality, the everydayness of life when we have to convert ideas into action. In the introduction, I prepared a list of responses that proved beneficial to congregations in the throes of change. The list is neither a step-by-step formula for instituting change nor a new model for tomorrow's church. Rather, it is about what we can expect in the change process; human behaviors, some that inhibit and some that stimulate; and addressing the challenges that accompany change. Even more, the list of responses is about mission and hope, and is a small witness that all—including ourselves, our congregations, and the entire cosmos—can become new in Christ. It's about our response to God's mission statement, "I am making everything new" (Rev. 21:5). But, all things, to become new, go through the wash. Laundry is everywhere.

A Laundry List

At the top of my laundry list, I noted the need for mature and motivated leaders in the congregation. Bowen Theory offers an alternative to leadership based on command and control or charisma—"the techniques of Moses." Murray Bowen's concept of leadership is more about influencing the emotional field or affecting the whole by one's essence and being. To convey his thinking, Bowen borrowed a term from embryology—*differentiation*. When a cell becomes something specific, such as a heart cell or a muscle cell, it is said to be differentiated. In contrast, a cell that remains nonspecific—a stem cell—is an immature cell. Differentiation, therefore, refers to maturity, which Bowen represented in the phrase "differentiation of self." Differentiation is a process in which a person's functioning is guided by a direction, supported by beliefs and values, and monitored by thoughtful behaviors rather than emotional reactivity. Differentiation is a range of functioning, never a set point. Different levels of anxiety, both internal and external, will test one's capacity to respond maturely.

Since life involves dealing with two basic needs—a separate self and a self connected to others—Bowen casts maturity in the form of a dialectic (two poles within a whole). The capacity to maintain the two forces as equal partners is a sign of maturity. But intrinsic to human functioning are two temptations: the temptation to distance from others and the temptation to dominate others or to dissolve self in relation to others. The former is called emotional cutoff. One can avoid the messiness of interactions by not being present. The other temptation is called emotional fusion, which is two sided: an individual could dominate others and make them extensions of himself or an individual could dissolve self by allowing someone else's functioning to determine hers.

Differentiation of self is a lifelong process of defining oneself and staying connected to others. A third capacity in the differentiating process is self-regulation—the ability to override one's own emotional reactivity and base behavior in principles or beliefs instead of instincts. Instinctive behavior is not learned; it comes with our DNA. We repeat the behavior. Unlike instinctive behavior, responsive behavior is learned. We encounter situations for which we have no ready-made response. At first, we rely on our old system of survival captained by the amygdala, the emotional appraisal system. The survival brain is preconscious, very rapid, and quite imprecise. It is not the most reliable part of the brain when novelty confronts us. It stirs up anxiety in the face of the strange or unknown. Anxiety stifles the imagination. Imaginative gridlock takes over; emotional barriers go uncontested. When anxious, our attention is on *conditions*, not *response*. We keep an eye on what is happening externally rather than reflecting on how we might respond. Instead of influencing the field by our calm reflectiveness and nonanxious behavior, we let the field influence our functioning.

One of the distinguishing capacities of our other brain—the thinking brain—is choosing how to respond. Intentionality trumps instinctiveness. As a consequence, we can make plans, create visions, and imagine what might come into being. We don't freeze in the moment of anxiety. Like Wagner Dodge, the firefighter at Mann Gulch, we stop running—the instinctive reaction—and think of something else to do.

Repeatedly, Edwin Friedman mentioned in his postgraduate seminars something to this effect: All these organizations with which I have consulted think they have their own special problem. But in every one of them, I see the same thing. It is the whiners, the complainers, the least imaginative, creative, and motivated who are calling the shots in those organizations. (Sometimes, he listed the most recalcitrant, the most immature, or the ones who take the least responsibility for their own well-being.) In short, Friedman indicts leaders who have had a failure of nerve, giving immediate and excessive attention to the NoNos.

No wonder that Friedman calls handling people's resistance "the key to the kingdom." He believed that mature functioning in a leader incites reactivity in the least mature. It is simply not possible to lead successfully through self-differentiation without inciting reactivity. The capacity of a leader to be aware of, to reflect upon, and to work through people's reactivity may be the most important aspect of leadership. It is "the key to the kingdom."

Immaturity has its payoffs. The immature quickly learn, "I can control a situation with bad behavior." Michael Jupin, an Episcopal priest and friend, sent me a cartoon in which a mother is holding the hand of her little daughter. The mother instructs the girl: "Remember, when life gives you lemons, be sure you pout, cry, and complain until life can't take the whining anymore and instead gives you cookies just to shut you up." When leaders become tyrannized by the cookie gouger, they function to soothe rather than to challenge—at the expense of progress.

In short, Friedman sees the challenge of change as producing sparks of anxious reactivity. Returning to the *HE* = *RO* formula, recall that the number and strength of the stressors (whining, negativity, critical words) are not to be the determining factor in how a healthy person responds. If you, the leader, do not overreact to anxiety, you will positively influence the emotional field. A minimum of reaction to others, especially the unmotivated, will not reinforce the sabotage. The challenge of change for leaders is to keep one's eye on the ball (stay focused), take the heat (remain nonreactive), stay connected (talk and listen), and get a good night's sleep.

The Change That Matters

Calm thoughtfulness can break the pattern of automatic behaviors. But the instinctive system is always ready to reclaim its dominance. The persistence of form is evident in the following two examples.

In 1803 the British established a position in which a designated person was to go to the cliffs of Dover and look for Napoleon. If Napoleon were sighted, the scout was to ring a bell. The job was not abolished for more than one hundred years. The persistence of form . . .

The combination of letters QWERTYUIOP is well known. Because of their crude mechanical design, the earliest typewriters would easily jam. To reduce the jamming, typewriter manufacturers redesigned the keyboard to make it a jumble of letters and thereby slow down the typist. But, when a new keyboard was developed in the early 1930s, one that made typing faster, manufacturers, teachers, and users resisted the change to a new arrangement. The persistence of form . . .

Change affects people in emotional ways, positively or negatively. Homeostasis—the known, the habitual, the reliable, the persistent—is incredibly powerful. So it should be, since it is a balancing mechanism. Who doesn't prefer patterns, habits, and the familiar over surprise, novelty, and confusion? People naturally give more power to the past (known) than to the future (unknown). A Jewish friend of mine reminded me that it took one year to get the Israelies out of Egypt, but forty years to get Egypt out of the Israelies. We like the familiar patterns, even as bad as they may be.

The positive side of homeostatic functioning is its provision of stability and equilibrium. The downside is its captivity to what has been—good or bad. Learning involves change—shuffling the deck, looking in strange places, exploring the neighborhood. "In times of crisis," historian Doris Kearns Goodwin states, "things become possible that would not be possible in ordinary times."[1] Crisis opens up the system. Familiar landmarks, directional arrows, and clear paths disappear. *Disorientation!* William Bridges reminded us that the neutral zone is precisely the time when innovation is most likely to happen and revitalization is possible.

Most churches in the neutral zone go into shock when they first arrive there. The psychic numbing is a temporary reprieve from confronting what has happened. There is too much laundry. As the anesthetic wears off, churches look outside themselves for help. Frustrated, congregations look for shortcuts, namely, transformation programs that promise quick relief. But shortcuts limit learning, which reminds me of Woody Allen's venture into speed reading. He said he read *War and Peace*. When asked what it is about, Allen replied, "Russia."

Today's church should not be looking outside itself or seeking the quick fix. First, a massive educational task is at hand. What do I mean? Church leaders have to reeducate people as to the purpose of the church. The purpose of the local church is not primarily to be one's church home or extended family, though it can be at times. And it is not to survive by obtaining more people for its support base. *Its purpose is to invite people to be part of the true mission of the church.* Reception into the church is only a threshold to involvement in its mission. The task of the church is not to accumulate attendees. The church is a school for developing agents of the new creation from among those who are the beneficiaries of God's grace.

Observing congregations over the years, I have noticed that the persistence of form generally gives way when the changes are connected to mission and sustained by hope. As strong as resistance may be, a counterforce exists that connects a clear direction with high expectations. Emotional systems not only resist but they can also choose to reinvigorate themselves. When leaders focus on opportunity and possibility, they unleash energy. Transforming emotional tension into creative tension takes a good deal of maturity—and patience. Overcoming the emotional barrier of "the church exists for me" is no overnight endeavor.

One of the most beneficial strategies I have discovered for freeing congregations stuck in their ways or frustrated by their decline is building what I will call the "mission school" into the congregation's life. I take twelve people into the school at a time. To raise awareness about mission, we focus on issues of the day and the biblical story. The awareness-raising includes participating in a project or experience the twelve choose. Then a second group of twelve is selected and trained. The focus is reversed from being served to becoming a servant. A congregation doesn't have to start big. Thomas Cahill, author of the Hinges of History series, including *How The Irish Saved Civilization*, notes, "No human group has ever figured out how to design its future. That future may be germinating today, not in a board room in London or an office in Washington or a bank in Tokyo, but . . . in some unheralded corner where a great-hearted human being is committed to loving outcasts in an extraordinary way."[2] An emotional system changes when people change how they function.

From the Ground Up

I am a strong believer in the "bubble up" concept. Successes from other sources cannot be easily replicated. Lyle Schaller, a highly respected church consultant and author, asks:

> What is the number-one issue facing Christian organizations on the North American continent today? . . . Dwindling numbers? Money? Social justice? Competent leadership? The growing dysfunctional nature of ecclesiastical structures? . . . After more than three decades spent working with thousands of congregational denominational, seminary, and parachurch leaders from more than five dozen tradi-

tions, this observer places a one-sentence issue at the top of that list. *The need to initiate and implement planned change from within an organization.*[3]

Anxious congregations either want relief from their pain or a stimulant to ignite their emotional fire. It is not surprising that the relief or stimulant they seek is to have someone become responsible for what they need. I, therefore, always begin my work with congregations repeating why I am present and what my responsibility is. In fact, I let them know I am not responsible for outcomes. I take responsibility for the process that will lead them to an outcome. Further, I inform them that they have the freedom not to learn from their own experience. They are responsible for the learning. Initially, many groups struggle with unimaginative ideas. With time, however, their learning ferments like good wine. Working from the ground up not only enables people to decide their own future but also reinforces their ability to do it. They utilize their own motivation and consequently see themselves less as victims. In turn, a burst of energy is released.

Reframe

The turnaround can be aided by reframing. Friedman encouraged the use of questions to "subvert mindsets," to rethink what has been assumed or practiced. He said the kind of questions we ask determine the kind of answers we receive. To jostle the mind, then, ask reverse questions. Instead of asking, "What can you do to improve the life of this congregation?" Friedman suggests asking, "What can you do to make this congregation extinct in twelve months?" Having tried this several times, I can assure you that the more serious people will give you incredulous looks. Sometimes, the look reads, "What can I do to make you extinct?" It takes a mature group to handle that question.

The subversive question actually functions in the same way as a reframe. To reframe is to look at something from another position, angle, or perspective, especially from a habitual position. Reframing can turn a negative point of view into its opposite.

Looking at the forms below, you see on the left side a random arrangement of four shapes. On the right, the same pieces are situated so that they form the letter *A*. This is a visual reframe.

People can also reframe their patterns of thinking. Imagine for a moment that your congregation is anticipating a significant change. In a public hearing, one leader concludes:

> We are a congregation that is dying. We have an old building needing repair and an older membership. How can we be called a "maintenance" church when we can't maintain what we have? Face it, we are a ghost of what we used to be. People don't want to come to a church of depressed folks. To try this change makes no sense at all. Get a grip on yourselves.

Meanwhile, a second leader puts the situation in a different light:

> We are a congregation in a neighborhood that is so different from the one that was here twenty years ago. We are no longer a large church. Yes, we struggle to stay afloat, but we can challenge ourselves more to rise above the problem. It's not clear to me how we will fare five to ten years from now. But it's a challenge. I'm committed to this congregation. What is keeping us from having lots of spirit, my friends, but our own selves?

The first speaker keeps pounding the stake of low expectations into the ground. It wouldn't take too much of the same negative talk to defeat any proposal about the future. Reframing the congregation's situation, the second speaker introduces hope and issues a challenge.

In a slightly different way, Jim Collins, noted for his work on how businesses go from "good to great," presents a reframe for any congregation to consider. When asked by people in the social sector what that passage might look like for them, Collins asserts that the social sectors are not to become more like business. Business, he claims, is focused on profit; the social sector, on the other hand, is based on service. Performance assessment in the social realm, therefore, is not dependent on financial returns or resources. The question for those in the social sector is, How effectively do we deliver on our mission and make a distinctive impact? To make a special impact, Collins says, social organizations must reframe; that is, they must focus on *outputs* (services), not *inputs* (receipts).[4]

The church, however, has typically focused on inputs: membership totals and gains, worship attendance averages, the amount of weekly offerings, additional physical space. The only output measurement is the amount given to benevolence, what some call "fair share" or judicatory assessments. Very seldom does one hear about the outputs. I wonder if the emphasis on inputs creates the impression that what people do for or give to the institution itself is the mission. I have found only one example in a church newsletter where the outputs were placed next to the inputs (offering and other sources of income). It looked like this:

THE KINGDOM OF GOD IS AMONG US

Three families are caring for another family member suffering from Alzheimer's. Two individuals, one from our congregation and one from another, help the three families weekly.

Seven of our members serve on boards of organizations that provide hope and healing to others.

Pastor will visit the McGrath Nursing Home this week to lead devotions.

Three of our youth are serving as their neighborhood reps for the American Cancer Society.

Let us all pray for the victims, the rescuers, and the healers who have been affected by this week's explosion.

Please remember to tell us about how our mission is happening through you in the world.

I think congregations encounter an emotional barrier in highlighting the inputs as what really counts and regarding the outputs as secondary or optional.

The Elephant in the Room

To think that outputs are as important as inputs may seem strange, because it's not what churches normally do. For example, when I presented the idea of God's new creation to a group of clergy, one participant objected to what I was proposing: "There's an elephant in the room that needs to be named." He thought that I had turned the church into a "gigantic welfare system." In addition, he heard me say that works precede faith and thought I had dressed the old social gospel in "a contemporary costume." Shouldn't he be suspicious of human "do goods" substituting for "the goodness of God?" he asked. I responded with a Mark Twain quip about salvation being by grace; otherwise, our dogs would get into heaven before us. Certainly, canine acts of obedience far surpass human efforts. Continuing, I said I believe the Reformers who insisted on the necessity of faith did not make good works its opposite. The opposite was faith in something other than the grace of God in Jesus Christ. They were careful to

say that the problem was *false opinions* about good works. Good
works don't set free; they have no re-creative power. In conclusion, I said faith is an *empowering connection,* for it cannot help
but become active in love. Grace becomes visible in our lives. Of
all people, Martin Luther—the great advocate for "grace alone"
and "faith alone"—repeated in his sermons:

> Afterwards—that is, after you have learned to believe in God's grace—
> think of nothing else except doing to your neighbor as Christ has
> done to you, and let all your works and your whole life be directed
> to your neighbor. Search out the poor, the sick, and every sort of
> needy person; help them; let the whole practice of your life consist
> in being helpful to them, to whoever needs you, as much as you are
> able, with body, goods, and honor.[5]

Luther did not set inputs and outputs as opposites. They are
all of a piece.

Put the Fish on the Table

Churches have a strong tendency to keep difficult things under
the table. Little changes because conflict-laden things are hidden. Of course, then, some laundry never gets done. George
Kohlrieser, a clinical psychologist and a hostage negotiator, has
been involved in life-and-death situations. Hostage negotiation
requires the ability to think fast and react slowly. To connect with
a hostage taker, Kohlrieser must act in a nonthreatening way,
for fear, generated by the amygdala and a powerful competitor
to logic and reason, has already set foot in the room. How does
one get past the stranglehold of emotionality? "Controlling
one's state, managing one's feelings, and using words—to ask
questions and seek a solution," Kohlrieser says, "is what hostage
negotiation is all about." In traumatic moments, emotional
reactions run wild, being disproportional to reality itself. A

hostage negotiator's own reactivity to a stressful situation will only maximize the shock.

Behind all hostage-taking situations, Kohlrieser saw a significant loss or a broken relationship in the recent history of the hostage taker. Feeling powerless, the hostage taker attempts to redress an injustice, to retaliate against any target available, and mostly to gain some control. What happens in these extreme circumstances, Kohlrieser claims, is the same as what happens in less stressful cases. Believing no options are left, the distraught give up hope. The deep anguish of a severed relationship locks down any thought of the future. When tomorrow is believed to be a painful repeat of today, a person has difficulty responding to fresh possibilities.

One day, when Kohlrieser was working in Sicily, he observed the fish market along the Mediterranean and the fishermen bringing the haul ashore and cleaning the fish. The fishermen invited the observer to join them. Dressed in an apron and with a knife in hand, he stood behind a long table. He heard someone give the instruction, "Put the fish on the table." What followed was a bloody mess. If the fish are left under the table, they begin to spoil, fester, and smell awful. So the cleaned fish are placed on ice. But Kohlrieser kept thinking to himself— "Put the fish on the table," realizing that is what must be done in hostage negotiation. Make the desperation visible, audible, palpable. Too many people opt for keeping the emotional stuff under the table. Surely, emotionally charged change can be a bloody mess. Aggression, hostility, distortion, rejection, and projection are some of the bloodstains. But without putting the fish on the table—and some gory mess—no super fish dinner will come later.[6]

Put the emotion on the table. Put the opposite viewpoints on the table. Put your questions on the table. Put the messiness that bedeviled you on the table. Put the losses on the table. We have been taught to keep the dirty laundry from public view. But without awareness, choice is impossible and it's back to the quiet days, the "see no evil" days. Transformations have *crisis* stamped on them. But it is not the crisis that will do a congregation in, it is the lack of *response* to the crisis. Place a frog in a kettle of boiling water and it will jump out. But you can kill it by putting the frog in the kettle and slowly raising the temperature of the water until the boiling point comes when no frog can survive. Congregations know "something isn't right" but go on and on and on like a frog in a slowly heating kettle. But, for heaven's sake, literally, people aren't frogs. We have choices.

Remembering the Future

Hope, we have been claiming, is a prime motive for Christian living. We can face adversity, oppositions, and setbacks because the present situation is never the last chapter for us. We are the new beginners.

Eschata is a Greek word meaning "last things." Eschatology is the study of last things. Eschatology is whatever one thinks about the future of human history, whether jihad, rapture, heaven, stargazing, palm reading, even fortune cookies. Eschatology is belief about the end time, whatever we anticipate will happen to the shape of things to come, whatever we are waiting for, whatever ultimate promise catches our imaginations. Eschatology is about where we have invested our hope.

Christian eschatology is the belief that the promises of God shape our lives here and now. The future influences the present, tomorrow affects today, anticipation informs action, and the morrow engages the moment. In an eschatological sense, the person who trusts the promises of God about the future need not be anxious about the next moment. Whenever one prays, "Thy kingdom come on earth as it is in heaven," we are in eschatological territory.

To understand this concept, let us revisit the past. For thirty-five hundred years, the Jews remembered God acting in history on their behalf. Through song and story, they recalled God liberating his people from the brutal brickyards of Pharaoh in Egypt. When new adversities appeared, the prophets urged the people to remember the Lord who brought them out of Egypt. Freedom, deeply etched in the Hebrew psyche, found its way into Christian thinking. The immense significance of the exodus event is evidenced in referring to Easter as "the second exodus." Remembering the mighty act of God, the apostle Paul speaks about the new exodus in which the whole creation will be set free from bondage and decay as it eagerly awaits the redemption of the sons and daughters of the earth. It is as if the entire universe has been under Pharaoh's foot. Likewise, Paul mentions the "groaning" of creation, which is reminiscent of the lamenting of the Israelites in their captivity. In another instance, the apostle refers to a freedom not from political shackles or exhausting labor but from sin and death for love and service.

Using Sydney Carter's prototype, we would say the whole creation, by God's grace, is set free from the "drag" for the "dance." God is moving all of life toward healing and restoration, toward experiences of joy and advocacy for justice, toward the freeing of captives and the feeding of the poor. One way to know something of this future is to recall what has happened before. Memory fortifies hope:

> But this I call to mind,
> And therefore I have hope:
> The steadfast love of the Lord never ceases,
> His mercies never come to an end;
> They are new every morning;
> Great is your faithfulness.
> "The Lord is my portion," says my soul,
> "Therefore, I will hope in him."

—LAMENTATIONS 3:21–24

As with the Jews, Christians base their hope through a memory system. "Remember Jesus Christ, raised from the dead" (2 Tim. 2:8a). Hope is grounded in God's faithfulness and promises.

With hope grounded in the expectation of a new world when all is forgiven, all is set free, all is restored, *the future is different*. A century ago, German theologian Ernst Troeltsch said that liberal churches had mostly closed the eschatological office. End-time talk held little interest. Among conservative churches, however, the eschatological office became a 24/7 matter. Fascination with the future has given birth to fanciful scenarios about time's grand finale, from holy wars to exact predictions, from a TV celebrity's injunction to rape the earth to the millennialist's suggestion that in the rapture drivers will leave their automobiles in traffic. But eschatology in biblical times was not about the end of a space-time world, not about the vanishing of the earth or its destruction, but about the transformation of this world. Our mission is not to save people out of this world but to prepare them for the new world. It is not about shutting doors; it is about seeing the door open. Eschatology shapes the mission around hope.

If the church is in a time of dislocation and disorientation (the exile), what will we do? Run away in Mann Gulch? Turn to the three temptations (denial, despair, and magic)? Stay in Plato's cave? Return to the chronic-helpless floor? Touch a small elephant? Succumb to Sanballat and other fear entrepreneurs? Leave our emotional bargains untested? Build bigger barns? Allow anxious moments to determine future direction?

Or will we hear the good news, trust the promises, attend to *tikkun olam,* connect mission with change, join the redeeming and repairing of the world so that it can become the good creation God intended, engage in hope fully confident that life need not stay the way it is, keep the light on at the eschatological office, and be the people of the way moving toward the door set open. You can make a difference.

A Meditation

Prayer

O God who has made us the creatures of time, so that every tomorrow is unknown country and every decision a venture of faith, grant us frail children of the day, who are blind to the future, to move toward it with a sure confidence in your love, from which neither life nor death can separate us.[1]

Verse

"See, I have placed before you an open door that no one can shut" (Rev. 3:8).

Reflection

Every now and then, we in the church need to step back and take a long view. God's kingdom is beyond our efforts, even our vision. In a lifetime, we participate in only a fraction of God's work. While we cannot do everything, we can do something. Incomplete as it may be, it is a step along the way, a beginning, and something for God to bless. God's grace does the rest. End results? We may never see them but only hold them trusting in God's future promises. We are servants, not saviors. We are ministers, not messianic figures. We are prophets of a future not of our own making but for which we hope and for which we make a defense in our life. We believe God will create a new heart in us and a new world out of the old.

Notes

Epigraph

G. K. Chesterton, "Xmas Day," in "The Notebook, 1894-97," *The Collected Works of G. K. Chesterton*, vol. 10 (San Francisco: Ignatius Press, 1994), 104.

Introduction

1. Anthony A. Hoekema, *The Bible and the Future* (Grand Rapids: William B. Eerdmans, 1979), 53.
2. Sarah S. Henrich, *Great Themes of the Bible*, vol. 2 (Louisville, KY: Westminster John Knox Press, 2007), 45.
3. Augustine, *Confessions*, bk. 1, pg. 1.

Part I: The Context

Walter Brueggemann, *Deep Memory, Exuberant Hope: Contested Truth in a Post-Christian World* (Minneapolis: Fortress Press, 2000), 29.

Chapter 1: There Once Was a World

1. Anthony B. Robinson, "Changing the Conversation: Nurturing a Third Way for Congregations," *Congregations*, Summer 2007, no. 3:2.
2. Phil Cousineau, ed., *The Way Things Are: Conversations with Huston Smith on the Spiritual Life* (Berkeley: University of California Press, 2003), 165.
3. Marc Auge, *Non-Places: Introduction to an Anthropology of Supermodernity* (London: Vego, 1995), 22, 27.

4. Cousineau, *The Way Things Are*, 150.

5. Bryan Appleyard, *Understanding the Present: Science and the Soul of Modern Man* (New York: Doubleday, 1993), 158.

6. Zack Lynch, *The Neuro Revolution: How Brain Science Is Changing Our World* (New York: St. Martin's Press, 2009), 157–158.

7. Hanna Rosin, "Did Christianity Cause the Crash?" *The Atlantic*, December 2009, 41.

8. Shirley Guthrie, *Journal of Pastoral Care* 31 (1977), quoted in "Theological Education for Emerging Ministries: Mentor Manual," Lutheran Seminary Program in the Southwest, 4; see www.lsps.edu/mentormanual.doc.

9. Joseph Bottum, "The Death of Protestant America: A Political Theory of the Protestant Mainline," *First Things*, August/September 2008, 24.

10. David T. Olson, *The American Church in Crisis* (Grand Rapids: Zondervan, 2008), 176.

11. Jon Meacham, "The End of Christian America," *Newsweek*, April 13, 2009, 38.

12. N. T. Wright, *Simply Christian: Why Christianity Makes Sense* (San Francisco: HarperSanFrancisco, 2006), 237.

13. Walter Brueggemann, *Deep Memory, Exuberant Hope: Contested Truth in a Post-Christian World* (Minneapolis: Fortress Press, 2000), 59.

Chapter 2: Emotional Systems and the New Anxiety

1. Barbara W. Tuchman, *A Distant Mirror: The Calamitous 14th Century* (New York: Alfred A. Knopf, 1978), 581.

2. Jonah Lehrer, *How We Decide* (New York: Houghton Mifflin Harcourt, 2009), 97.

3. Edwin H. Friedman, *Generation to Generation: Family Process in Church and Synagogue* (New York: Guilford Press, 1985), 24.

4. ———, *A Failure of Nerve: Leadership in the Age of the Quick Fix* (New York: Peabody Books, 2007), 246–247.

5. Ibid., 186.

6. Ibid., 214.

Chapter 3: So That You May Hope Again

1. Alan Deutschman, *Change or Die: The Three Keys to Change at Work and in Life* (New York: Regan, 2007), 11.

2. Ibid., 155.

3. Ibid., 14.

4. Walter Brueggemann, *Mandate to Difference: An Invitation to the Contemporary Church* (Louisville, KY: Westminster John Knox, 2007), 28–50.

5. Kosuke Koyama, *Mount Fuji and Mount Sinai: A Critique of Idols* (Maryknoll, NY: Orbis Books, 1984), 258.

6. Walter Brueggemann, *The Word Militant: Preaching a Decentering Word* (Minneapolis: Fortress Press, 2007), 132–33.

7. Leo Tolstoy, *What Is Art and Essays on Art* (Oxford: Oxford University Press, 1930), variant quoted in James Gleick, *Chaos: Making a New Science* (New York: Penguin Books, 1987), 38.

8. T. S. Eliot, *The Rock* (New York: Harcourt, Brace, 1934).

9. John Kotter, *Our Iceberg Is Melting* (New York: St. Martin's Press, 2006), 86ff.

10. Ellen J. Langer, *Counterclockwise: Mindful Health and the Power of Possibility* (New York: Ballantine Books, 2009), 106–7.

11. Kosuke Koyama, *Three Mile an Hour God* (Maryknoll, NY: Orbis Books, 1979), 18.

12. Charles Peguy "The Portal of the Mystery of Hope" (Grand Rapids: Eerdmans, 1996), quoted in Ben Birnbaum, ed., *Take Heart: Catholic Writers on Hope in Our Time* (New York: Crossroads, 2007), 67.

Part II: The Mission

N. T. Wright, *Simply Christian: Why Christianity Makes Sense* (San Francisco: HarperSanFrancisco, 2006), 204.

Carl E. Braaten, *The Apostolic Imperative: Nature and Aim of the Church's Mission and Ministry* (Minneapolis: Augsburg, 1985), 78.

David J. Bosch, *Transforming Mission: Paradigm Shifts in Theology of Mission* (Maryknoll, NY: Orbis Books, 2006), 414.

Chapter 4: The Challenge of Change

1. Anne Lamott, *Plan B: Further Thoughts on Faith* (New York: Riverhead Books, 2005), 221.

2. Edwin Friedman (lecture, postgraduate seminar on family emotional process, Bethesda, Maryland, 1993).

3. Ibid.

4. Annie Dillard, *Pilgrim at Tinker Creek: A Mystical Excursion into the Natural World* (New York: Bantam Books, 1974), 26.

5. Ibid., 31.

6.   Carol Kinsey Goman, "The Ten Biggest Mistakes We Made Managing Change . . . And the Lessons We Learned," Kinsey Consulting Services, http://www.ckg.com/archive3.html (accessed November 2009).

7.   George A. Akerlof and Robert J. Shiller, *Animal Spirits: How Human Psychology Drives the Economy and Why It Matters for Global Capitalism* (Princeton, NJ: Princeton University Press, 2009), 3, 55, 167.

8.   I have reworked Kotter's chart to fit the church. See John Kotter, "Leading Change: Why Transformation Efforts Fail," *Harvard Business Review OnPoint,* Executive Edition, March–April 1995.

9.   John P. Kotter, *A Sense of Urgency* (Boston: Harvard Business Press, 2008), viii.

10.   Kathleen Norris, *Dakota: A Spiritual Geography* (New York: Houghton Mifflin, 1993), 165.

11.   David Augsburger, *Dissident Discipleship: A Spirituality of Self-Surrender, Love of God, and Love of Neighbor* (Grand Rapids: Brazos Press, 2006), 185, 186.

Chapter 5: The Making of a Mission Culture

1.   William Sheldon, quoted in Huston Smith, *Why Religion Matters: The Fate of the Human Spirit in an Age of Disbelief* (San Francisco: Harper, 2001), 26.

2.   David Brooks, "The Power of Posterity," *New York Times*, July 27, 2009, repr. *Austin-American Statesman*, July 30, 2009.

3.   Craig Van Gelder, *The Ministry of the Missional Church: A Community Led by the Spirit* (Grand Rapids: Baker Books, 2007), 18.

4.   David Bosch, *Transforming Mission: Paradigm Shifts in Theology of Mission* (Maryknoll, NY: Orbis Books, 2006), 412.

5.   Paul S. Minear, *Images of the Church in the New Testament* (Louisville, KY: Westminster John Knox, 2004), 29ff.

6.   N. T. Wright, *Surprised by Hope: Rethinking Heaven, the Resurrection, and the Mission of the Church* (New York: HarperOne, 2008), 270.

7.   Ibid.

Chapter 6: Joining God's New Creation

1.   N. T. Wright, *Surprised by Hope: Rethinking Heaven, the Resurrection, and the Mission of the Church* (New York: HarperOne, 2008), 192.

2.   Benedict XVI, *On Christian Hope: Encyclical Letter* (Washington, DC: United States Conference of Catholic Bishops, 2007), 3.

3. Leon H. Cheney, *The Mystery of the Kaddish: Its Profound Influence on Judaism* (Fort Lee, NJ: Barricade Books, 2006), xviii.

4. Paul Althaus, *The Theology of Martin Luther*, trans. Robert C. Schultz (Philadelphia: Fortress Press, 1966), 424.

5. N. T. Wright, *Simply Christian: Why Christianity Makes Sense* (San Francisco: HarperSanFrancisco, 2006), xi.

6. Jurgen Moltmann, *In the End—The Beginning: The Life of Hope* (Minneapolis: Augsburg Fortress, 2004), 160.

7. Joel B. Green, *Body, Soul, and Human Life: The Nature of Humanity in the Bible* (Grand Rapids: Baker Academic, 2008), 180.

8. William C. Placher, ed., *Essentials of Christian Theology* (Louisville, KY: Westminster John Knox, 2003), 354.

9. Richard John Neuhaus, *American Babylon: Notes of a Christian Exile* (New York: Basic Books, 2009), 246.

10. Carl Henry and John Stott, quoted in David Bosch, *Transforming Mission: Paradigm Shifts in Theology of Mission* (Maryknoll, NY: Orbis Books, 2006), 404, 405.

11. H. Russel Botman, "Hope as the Coming Reign of God," in *Hope for the World: Mission in a Global Context*, ed. Walter Brueggemann (Louisville, KY: Westminster John Knox, 2001), 78.

12. Lois Y. Barrett and others, *Treasure in Clay Jars: Patterns in Missional Faithfulness* (Grand Rapids: Eerdmans, 2004), 60, 61.

13. Rick Warren, *The Purpose Driven Church: Growth Without Compromising Your Message and Mission* (Grand Rapids: Zondervan, 1995), 6.

14. N. T. Wright, *Surprised by Hope*, 208.

Part III: The Response

N. T. Wright, *Simply Christian: Why Christianity Makes Sense*, (San Francisco: HarperSanFrancisco, 2006), 92.

Chapter 7: The People of the Way

1. Annie Dillard, *Pilgrim at Tinker Creek: A Mystical Excursion into the Natural World* (New York: Bantam Books, 1974), 2, 12.

2. Jay Griffiths, *A Sideways Look at Time* (New York: Jeremy P. Tarcher/Putnam, 1999), 245.

3. Carla Hannaford, *Smart Moves: Why Learning Is Not All in Your Head* (Arlington, VA: Great Ocean Publishers, 1995), 96.

4. Sydney Carter, *Green Print for Song* (London: Galliard/Stainer & Bell, 1974).

5. William H. Willimon, *Undone by Easter: Keeping Preaching Fresh* (Nashville: Abingdon, 2009), 29.

6. William Bridges, *The Way of Transition: Embracing Life's Most Difficult Moments* (Cambridge, MA: Perseus Publishing, 2001), 219.

7. Edwin H. Friedman, *A Failure of Nerve: Leadership in the Age of the Quick Fix* (New York: Peabody Books, 2007), 97ff.

8. Bridges, *Way of Transition*, 129.

9. Friedman, *Failure of Nerve*, 251.

10. Isaac Watts, 1674–1748.

Chapter 8: Where to Touch the Elephant

1. Edwin Friedman (lecture, postgraduate seminar on family emotional process, Bethesda, Maryland, 1993).

2. Howard Thurman, "The Work of Christmas," in *The Mood of Christmas and Other Celebrations* (Richmond, IN: Friends United Press, 1985), 23. Used by permission of the publisher.

3. N. T. Wright, *Surprised by Hope* (New York: HarperOne, 2008), 193.

4. Loren Eiseley, *The Unexpected Universe* (New York: Harcourt, Brace, and World, 1969), 67ff.

5. Desmond Tutu (sermon, All Saints Church, Pasadena, CA, May 23, 1999).

Chapter 9: A Different Future

1. Diane Coutu, "Leadership Lessons from Abraham Lincoln: A Conversation with Historian Doris Kearns Goodwin," *Harvard Business Review*, April 2009.

2. Thomas Cahill, *How the Irish Saved Civilization: The Story of Ireland's Heroic Role from the Fall of Rome to the Rise of Medieval Europe* (New York: Doubleday, 1995), 217.

3. Lyle E. Schaller, *Strategies for Change* (Nashville: Abingdon, 1993), cover.

4. Jim Collins, *Good to Great and the Social Sectors: Why Business Thinking Is Not the Answer* (Boulder, CO: Jim Collins, 2005), 4–5.

5. Martin Luther, quoted in Heinrich Bornkamm, *The Heart of Reformation Faith: The Fundamental Axioms of Evangelical Belief* (New York: Harper and Row, 1965), 29.

6. George Kohlrieser, *Hostage at the Table: How Leaders Can Overcome Conflict, Influence Others, and Raise Performance* (San Francisco: Jossey-Bass, 2006), 108, 109.

Epilogue

1. Reinhold Niebuhr, quoted in Douglas John Hall, *The Future of the Church: Where Are We Headed?* (Toronto: United Church Publishing House, 1989), 69.